TALENTED

TALENTED

DISCOVERING *AND* USING YOUR GOD-GIVEN TALENTS TO *FIND* **MORE JOY** IN LIFE

DUSTIN PETERSON

CFI
An imprint of Cedar Fort, Inc.
Springville, Utah

ISBN 13: 978-1-4621-4043-5

Published by CFI, an imprint of Cedar Fort, Inc.
2373 W. 700 S., Springville, UT 84663
Distributed by Cedar Fort, Inc., www.cedarfort.com

Library of Congress Control Number: 2021933586

Cover design by Shawnda T. Craig

Printed in the United States of America

10 9 8 7 6 5 4 3 2 1

Printed on acid-free paper

To Samye, the most talented and Christlike person I know.

Contents

Acknowledgments

The great paradox of talents is this: those things we are most natural at doing are the things we are often most self-conscious to do. Perhaps it's that the things we love are so closely tied to our identity, but I find time and again that the things of my soul that I most want to share are the things I guard most closely. This book is one of those things.

For five years I tinkered and tweaked the manuscript for this book, often wondering if it would be of any value. Alas, the only way to find out is to do as my friend Aaron Smith once said, "Just publish the book already!"

This book would not exist without the support and constant encouragement from my eternal companion, Samye, who has been and always will be my greatest supporter. She believes in me and in my talents more than I believe in myself.

Lindsey Thaler is my personal editor extraordinaire who laid eyes on this project more than two years ago and said this book was special and important. It was her motivating comments and affirmation that gave me the boost I needed to write it.

Special thanks to Lindsay Broadbent for allowing me to tell her story, to Randy Macchi and Ray Holt for being the kind of people who magnify their talents without seeking attention or praise, and for the many clients, listeners, and others who trust my advice and counsel to guide them on their journey and whose stories lend credibility to this book.

I'll be forever grateful to Kurt Francom for giving me a platform to share content I love, Matt Broadbent and Ryan Nelson for their constant inspiration and support, and Bryce Wong for teaching an inspired class on talents many years that sparked my interest in studying the topic more deeply. Also thank you to Shaun Chidester, who believed in my teaching ability and cleared the path for me to pursue my talents.

Thank you to my talented children, parents, in-laws, and family, who are the greatest cheerleaders of the work I do. No one develops their talents in a vacuum.

I'm especially appreciative of the great folks at Cedar Fort Publishing for those magical words, "We love it and would like to publish it!" Talents often stay hidden without encouragement from those with the platform, resources, and power to bring them to light. The Cedar Fort team did that for me.

And thank you to you, the reader, for taking the risk to learn more about who God intended for you to be. Discover what you do best and do more of it. We, the world, are waiting for you!

CHAPTER 1

That They Might Have Joy

"Jesus knew who he was and why he was here on this planet. That meant he could lead from strength rather than from uncertainty or weakness."[1]

—PRESIDENT SPENCER W. KIMBALL

You don't know who you are.

You may think you know, but you don't *really* know.

But you're not alone. Most of us don't fully comprehend who we are and what we are capable of.

Each of us came into this world with a unique set of abilities, traits, and talents given to us by our Heavenly Father—things that set us apart from other people. No two people were created with exactly the same abilities. All are unique. When we were born, we brought these gifts, talents, and abilities with us. We may recognize some of these gifts, or they may lie dormant within us. And yet, when asked to identify and describe these "gifts," we are generally stumped.

This point was reaffirmed to me a number of years ago in an elders quorum meeting at church. The lesson was "Developing and Utilizing Talents," and the teacher had chosen to open with a question. He asked the quorum to start off by sharing some of their talents.

"Raise your hand, if you will, and share a talent with the quorum—something that you feel is a talent for you." Because of my research on this topic I sat up a little straighter in my chair, interested to hear the responses.

Silence.

The instructor shifted a bit, adjusting his notes, and patiently embraced the awkward silence. A few men began looking around while others stared at the floor. Some guy coughed to break the silence. Finally, one brother raised his hand. You could feel the pressure release from the room like pressing a valve on a tire tube.

Everyone turned to the man, waiting for his response. "I'm really good at being humble," he said. "In fact, I'm the most humble person I know . . . It just comes naturally to me." The group chuckled and the mood lightened. Another man raised his hand. "Can I share someone else's talent? Lyle is a really good photographer and one of the more creative people I know," he said, pointing to another of the men in the room.

The teacher affirmed this statement and then asked one last time. No one responded, and so the instructor shared some of his talents. He said he was good at athletics and has always been a pretty competitive guy. He followed up this statement by saying something like, "I guess that's a talent." And then we moved on with the lesson. I felt empty. This was a room full of committed and faithful priesthood holders, and yet the only thing we could come up with for strengths was "photography" and "athleticism." How was this possible? How could a room full of young-to-middle-aged men teeming with talent only generate a few responses? Was it fear? Lack of self-awareness? More important, if this group of thirty men felt this way, how did their wives and children feel about their own talents? Do people around the world know what their God-given gifts are and how to breathe life into them?

I say enough is enough. The Lord expects us to identify our talents, develop them, and put them to use. In *Jesus the Christ,* Elder James E. Talmage said, "Likewise, in the spiritual application, a man possessed of any good gift, such as musical ability, eloquence, skill in handicraft, or the like, ought to use that gift to the full, that he or others may be profited thereby; but should he be too neglectful to exercise his powers in independent service, he may assist others to profitable effort, by encouragement if by nothing more."[2]

You should understand what your talents are and use them "to the full"! Or, at the very least, you should help other people identify theirs, including your husband or wife, son or daughter, counselor in your presidency, or your Primary children. This self-knowledge of talents is powerful. In fact, it is the key to immediately improving our lives in so many ways. I have seen this knowledge of talents pay huge dividends in choosing a career, leading an organization, parenting more effectively, or serving in the Church. I have also seen the dark side of not knowing who you are.

In 2004, I had just graduated from BYU–Idaho. Throughout my college career I had struggled to nail down my talents or a best-fit major, for that matter. Thus, after exploring and formally registering seven different majors over the course of five years (likely a record at BYU–Idaho), I landed in communications, specializing in public relations. After graduation, my wife and I relocated to Dallas, Texas, and I did exactly what society prescribes: got a job and became a breadwinner. I landed a job at a public relations firm and almost immediately began dreading work. My job was totally incongruent with me to the point that I began to fall into depression. I felt tired all the time. In fact, I was so down about my job that I had my morning routine planned out down to the minute so that I didn't have to spend an additional second thinking about work. The alarm would go off at 7:45 a.m. and I'd pull the sheets over my head in denial (my wife called it "going into Dustin world"). I'd leap out of bed at 7:52 a.m., shower, and hit the door by 8:08 a.m. with breakfast in hand to put me in the office before 9 a.m.

I worked on the healthcare and hospitality team at the agency, meaning that I coordinated press releases and media requests for a hotel chain and our healthcare-related clients. I'll never forget my first week on the job. I was brought into a meeting and told that we were launching a media campaign to generate attention for one of our big brands and I was going to take lead on calling media to pitch the idea of them covering our client. Big responsibility. Then they dropped the bomb. The client was Beano. Yes, *that* Beano—as in the pill people take to fight bloating and gas. My boss told me that I was being tasked with calling major media publications—think *Good Housekeeping* and *Oprah Magazine*—and announcing the release of a landmark research study showing that more than 10 million Americans every year suffer from complex carbohydrate intolerance: when you eat beans you get gas. And Beano can help!

I thought for sure this was a joke. I looked around the table waiting for someone to crack, but all I got in return were serious looks. The mood in the room felt intense, like we were curing cancer or launching a spaceship to the moon. So, I did what any young, motivated employee would do. I dutifully accepted the assignment, grabbed my call list of around seventy-five major publications, and holed up in a call booth to conquer the world of mass media, one pitch at a time.

These calls drained my soul. Each call was met with rejection, mid-sentence hang-ups, and some choice words from a few executive editors. I didn't remember studying this aspect of public relations at BYU–Idaho. I must have been out that week.

Day after day I returned to my call booth to take a heavy dose of rejection. At the end of each day I reported my lack of success to my manager with true sadness. She would act surprised and encourage me to keep trying. Someone was bound to be interested in a story about gas.

Then I called Doug.

Doug was the executive editor of a major fitness publication. We're talking "industry leading." The stakes felt high. I made the call, listened to the ringing on the other end of the line, and sprang to life when he picked up the phone.

"This is Doug."

"Hi, Doug, I'm calling on behalf of Beano." I paused to wait for him to chew me out or hang up. Neither happened, so I continued. "Did you know that 10 million Americans suffer from complex carbohydrate intolerance every year? And Beano can help!" Again, I waited. A long, painful pause ensued. I could hear the low din of phones ringing and people working in the background. Then Doug spoke up.

"Dustin," he said, clearing his throat. "Are we talking about farts?"

I stumbled. "Uh . . . well, kind of . . . I mean . . . "

"Dustin," he said again, "do yourself a favor. Don't ever call me again. And go figure out something different to do with your life."

Click.

Now, I was used to rejection. I had served a mission for the Church and had taken my fair share of rejection over two years. But this one stung, likely because he was right.

What was I doing with my life? I had been isolated in a call booth for days—even weeks—trying to convince major media outlets to cover gas. Is this what I got a degree to do? Is this what God intended for me? Was this the plan?

Some of you may have felt this with your work, this incongruence that makes you feel tired, weak, de-energized, or lost. Others may feel it in their church assignment, volunteer activities, or even home life. You might ask, "What am I doing?" or "Why this?" or "Is this it? Is this what Father in Heaven has in store for me?"

At the time, I couldn't figure out why life felt so low. I remember thinking, "Man, why is this so painful? Why is this so hard for me? Why do I feel so sluggish and drained all the time?" I felt that inner tension between doing my duty as a breadwinner for my family and absolutely hating what I was doing day-in and day-out. I wondered if I should just buck up. Maybe this is what work was all about. Surely there were people doing worse things than this for work. Shouldn't I be grateful? Maybe I should just put my head down and press on.

I felt lost and in desperate need of some heavenly intervention. In the course of feeling this, I came across two passages of scripture that shaped my entire career. In fact, these scriptures changed my whole trajectory and set me on the path I'm on today. They form the foundation for this book and my discovery of talents.

I was sitting on the edge of the bed one morning reading the scriptures. I felt scattered in my personal study and decided just to flip open the scriptures and read wherever I landed. I turned to this first scripture and read 2 Nephi 2:25: "Adam fell that men might be; and **men are, that they might have joy**" (emphasis added).

This verse hit me to the core. I froze and stared up at the wall. I thought, "YES! Men are that they might have joy! Not "that they might have joy from 5 p.m. to 10 p.m. and then again until work starts the next day." Or "that they might have joy on Saturday and Sunday but take a flogging the rest of the days." I realized that "men are that they might have joy" every day, even at work. So, if I'm miserable in my work, there's got to be something I can do about it. It's not meant to be this way!

A good friend of mine, Lindsey, made an interesting point in reference to this verse. She said, "I love this. It runs a little bit counter to what society would tell you. Like, I feel like there's pressure for people to prove how much hardship they've endured as if that makes them more legit humans. But this verse says nothing about that. It just says you exist; therefore, you may have joy." I felt the same when I read it fifteen years ago, and I feel it now. God intends for us to have joy, and I knew that day that His promise held true for me.

I sometimes hear people say things like, "It's called 'work' for a reason!" or "It's supposed to be hard." To be clear, I agree that work can be hard. Father Adam was told that "in the sweat of thy face shalt thou eat bread, till thou return unto the ground" (Genesis 3:19). What I don't see in that verse is "through misery thou shalt eat bread" or "in pain, boredom, and disengagement shalt thou eat bread." Rather, I believe we can find joy in any circumstance, and I realized in the moment that I read these verses that this was God's intent for me.

But how? How can we love work or chores or the tedium of day-to-day life? How can we maximize the "9 to 5"? How can we find meaning, even in difficult circumstances?

On that same morning of scripture study, I cross-referenced "joy" over to these verses from Matthew 25:14–29, otherwise referred to as the parable of the talents, and found my answer to the previous question. I've bolded several statements that had tremendous impact on me:

> For the kingdom of heaven is as a man travelling into a far country, who called his own servants, and delivered unto them his goods.

And unto one he gave five talents, to another two, and to another one; **to every man according to his several ability**; and straightway took his journey.

Then he that had received the five talents went and traded with the same, and made them other five talents.

And likewise he that had received two, he also gained other two.

But he that had received one went and digged in the earth, and hid his lord's money.

After a long time the lord of those servants cometh, and reckoneth with them.

And so he that had received five talents came and brought other five talents, saying, Lord, thou deliveredst unto me five talents: behold, **I have gained beside them five talents more.**

His lord said unto him, **Well done, thou good and faithful servant**: thou hast been faithful over a few things, I will make thee ruler over many things: **enter thou into the joy of thy lord.**

He also that had received two talents came and said, Lord, thou deliveredst unto me two talents: behold, I have gained two other talents beside them.

His lord said unto him, **Well done, good and faithful servant**; thou hast been faithful over a few things, I will make thee ruler over many things: **enter thou into the joy of thy lord.**

Then he which had received the one talent came and said, Lord, I knew thee that thou art an hard man, reaping where thou hast not sown, and gathering where thou hast not strawed:

And **I was afraid, and went and hid thy talent in the earth:** lo, there thou hast that is thine.

His lord answered and said unto him, **Thou wicked and slothful servant, thou knewest that I reap where I sowed not, and gather where I have not strawed:**

Thou oughtest therefore to have put my money to the exchangers, and then at my coming I should have received mine own with usury.

Take therefore the talent from him, and give it unto him which hath ten talents.

For unto every one that hath shall be given, and he shall have abundance: but from him that hath not shall be taken away even that which he hath.

I read this parable and several things hit me:

1. He gave talents to "every man (and woman) according to his (or her) several ability." Not most people—everyone! So, if you're reading this book and aren't yet convinced that you have talents, this parable is for you!
2. You can gain more talents. One of these servants gained five more and the other gained two.
3. Talents lead to the joy of the Lord. This is key. If "men are that they might have joy," then how do I access that joy? At least one way lies in developing and maximizing your God-given talents. And what is the "joy of the Lord"? Long-term, it's eternal life, the joy that comes from living together with our families in the presence of God. But in the short-term it's the feelings of peace, contentment, happiness, energy, control, and confidence that come from aligning your will to His. It's the sum total of goodness that comes from the Savior as a byproduct for using the talents He's blessed us with to bring joy to those around us.
4. When we're afraid, we tend to bury our talents and hide what we do best. We'll discuss why later on, but for now it's important to recognize that we can likely relate with and feel empathy for the servant who buried his talents, knowing the risk that would come with multiplying them.
5. If we don't discover and use them, we lose them! This one makes my palms sweat. God has endowed us with talents that yield tremendous outcomes for us and those within our circle of influence. To bury them is to forsake the heavenly gift. God can't have those gifts go for naught and so He will re-assign them where they'll be most productively used. Use it or lose it!

So much packed into so few verses! And yet, more than anything on that morning during those ten minutes of scripture study, I walked away thinking, "So . . . I must have talents, they must lead me to more joy if I use them, and I must be either burying them or ignoring them; otherwise I wouldn't feel the way I feel." I felt like the clouds had parted. The clear message was that I could have joy, even at work, and that joy came from identifying and using my talents. Moreover, I likely was not currently using my talents and was running a joy deficit as a result.

This passage was like a lightning bolt to my soul. I felt *compelled* to discover my talents and put them to use. I absolutely believed these talents would take me to a place of more joy in the Lord, and I was committed to do whatever it took to figure them out. I sat in the car on my commute that day with one big question on my mind: "What are my talents, and how do I discover them?"

The journey was long, and it would be several more years before I'd truly hone in on my talents and put them to use on a daily basis, but the results have been incredible. Since that day sixteen years ago, I've worked in more than a dozen jobs, completed a master's degree, and built a business around leading executives to discover what they do best and do more of it. I've coached, taught, and trained thousands of individuals to identify and maximize their gifts through ThePurposeBlueprint.com. I've led in the Church and in my family. Most important, I've become more of who God intended for me to be, and I've felt the peace that comes with congruence and authenticity. I want to help you feel the same.

TAKE HEART AND HAVE COURAGE

You are meant to have joy! Like, today. Not in the future, not from sixty-five years old on, and certainly not only in the next life. And one source of joy is the use and magnification of talents.

It turns out, the core of figuring out what to do with your life is knowing who you are. This knowledge is integral to everything from parenting to fulfilling a calling. We can use what we know about ourselves to guide us in major decisions, to capitalize on opportunities the Lord puts in our path, and to find increased joy in life.

The irony is that for most of us this knowledge lies just out of reach. We have the ability to determine who we are and what we should be doing with our lives, and how we should be doing it, but we just don't know how to access that knowledge or use that power.

Why is that? Why don't we know our talents?

I have to believe—and frequently teach—that no one got left out of the talent lottery in the premortal life. Everyone has them. It's not like we were lining up for talents before this life and you stepped out to grab a sandwich and got passed up.

Everyone has them.

Part of the reason we have a difficult time articulating our talents is that we don't know what we are looking for. We tend to look at talents as tangible things. It's easy to see a prolific basketball player, painter, musician, or dancer and recognize their tangible gift. It's much more difficult to identify intangible gifts, even if the gifts are equally as important.

My wife asked our daughter one morning what talents she thought she had. After a long pause, my daughter said, "Playing the piano, I guess." My wife prodded her to come up with another one. "Dance?" My wife said that she thought Halle's ability to make other people laugh was a talent.

I thought this was so indicative of each of us. We only see activities with tangible outputs as talents. And yet, Elder Marvin J. Ashton of the Quorum of the Twelve Apostles taught this powerful principle in his talk entitled "There Are Many Gifts." He said,

> Let me mention a few gifts that are not always evident or noteworthy but that are very important. Among these may be your gifts—gifts not so evident but nevertheless real and valuable. Let us review some of these less-conspicuous gifts: the gift of asking; the gift of listening; the gift of hearing and using a still, small voice; the gift of being able to weep; the gift of avoiding contention; the gift of being agreeable; the gift of avoiding vain repetition; the gift of seeking that which is righteous; the gift of not passing judgment; the gift of looking to God for guidance; the gift of being a disciple; the gift of caring for others; the gift of being able to ponder; the gift of offering prayer; the gift of bearing a mighty testimony; and the gift of receiving the Holy Ghost.[3]

Can you feel the power of his statement? Not all gifts are easily observable and, therefore, easy to identify. But that certainly doesn't mean they "don't count." Each of us has talents. Perhaps you even identified a few of yours in Elder Ashton's quote. You may also have people come to mind who possess these gifts. I can think of people for each of them and the way they magnify those talents for the benefit of humankind.

And not only do we have these gifts, but we are expected to *use them.* It's a commandment.

In June of 1965, a group of brethren in the Physical Facilities Department of the Church was doing some work outside the Hotel Utah apartment of President David O. McKay. As President McKay stopped to explain to them the importance of the work in which they were engaged, he paused and told them the following:

> Let me assure you, Brethren, that someday you will have a personal priesthood interview with the Savior, Himself. If you are interested, I will tell you the order in which He will ask you to account for your earthly responsibilities.
>
> First, He will request an accountability report about your relationship with your wife. Have you actively been engaged in making her happy and ensuring that her needs have been met as an individual?
>
> Second, He will want an accountability report about each of your children individually. He will not attempt to have this for simply a family stewardship report but will request information about your relationship to each and every child.
>
> Third, He will want to know what you personally have done with the talents you were given in the premortal world.

Whoa, stop there for a second. Third?! Like, right after wife and kids? Not callings or stewardship of resources or temple attendance? Not missionary work? *Talents*?

For those who are curious, I'll finish the quote:

> Fourth, He will want a summary of your activity in your Church assignments. He will not be necessarily interested in what assignments you have had, for in His eyes the home teacher

> and mission president are probably equals, but He will request a summary of how you have been of service to your fellowmen in your Church assignments.
>
> Fifth, He will have no interest in how you earned your living, but if you were honest in all your dealings.
>
> Sixth, He will ask for an accountability on what you have done to contribute in a positive manner to your community, state, country, and the world.[4]

People often cite number five as a reason to just work a job for the sake of working. "God doesn't really care what you do for a living." But note that He *does* care about whether you maximized your talents, and your day-to-day work is certainly a place where that happens, regardless of what you do from 9 a.m. to 5 p.m.

So why *would* talents be number three? At least one reason may be that talents are the tools He's given us to bless our lives and facilitate the journey home of all of His children. Reflecting on Elder Ashton's quote above, who wouldn't be benefited in their journey back to our Heavenly Parents by a friend or family member gifted in listening, caring, or not judging another? Which of us wouldn't want to be surrounded by gifted empathizers, testifiers, or family members who are in tune with the Holy Ghost on our course back to our heavenly home?

It seems like it would be pretty important to figure these out. This is the goal of this book. I first want to address at length what talent is and why we don't know our talents. We'll then dive into three categories of talents and how to discover them. We'll finish by talking about how to grow them, apply them, and help others discover them. Throughout the book, I'll share examples, anecdotes, and activities to guide your discovery of talents. And the big promise of this book—my hope for you—is that you walk away more empowered to know who you are, what you do best, and how to do more of it to find more joy in life.

I've found three main challenges around talents:

1. We don't know we even have them.
2. If we know we have them, we don't know how to identify or articulate them.

3. Even if we're willing and able to identify them, we won't share them!

I received an email recently from a woman in Utah who had listened to a podcast I did for Leading Saints on "Leading with Your Talents." She said:

> I have learned more about myself and the talents I have over the last ten years but there were, and still are, times of feeling 'talentless.' I recognize that there are many women (and men!) who feel similarly, especially when a lot of personal pursuits can be put on hold for family. I recognize I have many talents I can and do use in raising my children, organizing and running my home, and cultivating a strong marriage. I believe Satan tries so hard to make mothers feel useless and talentless in fulfilling their role as a mother.

She's right. The adversary actively attacks our identity and in particular those aspects of who we are that make us unique and special in the eyes of the Lord.

By the end of this book, my hope is that you discover your own uniqueness—your God-given talents—and that you have a clear path to develop them for the benefit of humankind. I hope to put a dent in the notion of being "talentless."

Elder Joseph B. Wirthlin of the Quorum of the Twelve Apostles said, "The Lord did not people the earth with a vibrant orchestra of personalities only to value the piccolos of the world. Every instrument is precious and adds to the complex beauty of the symphony. All of Heavenly Father's children are different in some degree, yet each has his own beautiful sound that adds depth and richness to the whole."[5]

We all have them. Let's figure them out.

NOTES

1. Spencer W. Kimball, "Jesus, The Perfect Leader." *Ensign*, Aug. 1979, churchofjesuschrist.org/study/ensign/1979/08/jesus-the-perfect-leader?lang=eng.
2. James E. Talmage, *Jesus the Christ: A Study of the Messiah and His Mission According to Holy Scriptures Both Ancient and Modern* (Salt Lake City: Deseret Book, 1963).

3. Marvin J. Ahston, "There are Many Gifts." *Ensign*, Nov. 1987, churchofjesuschrist.org/study/general-conference/1987/10/there-are-many-gifts?lang=eng.
4. Robert D. Hales, "Understandings of the Heart," BYU devotional March 1988, Speeches.byu.edu.
5. Joseph B. Wirthlin, "Concern for the One," *Ensign,* May 2008, churchofjesuschrist.org/study/general-conference/2008/04/concern-for-the-one?lang=eng.

CHAPTER 2

The Enemies of Talent

"We develop our talents first by thinking we can."[1]

—JAMES E. FAUST

Awhile back I was asked to speak to a group of young women ages twelve to eighteen about their God-given talents. I started like this:

"What is a talent?"

Hands went up.

"Something that makes you different!"

"A unique power!"

"A trait that helps you do stuff other people can't do!"

Nailed it. I once taught a group of sixth graders and asked them the same question. One raised their hand and said, "A superpower!" Wow. Dead on.

I then asked these young women to raise their hand if they have a talent.

No hands went up.

Not one young woman felt like she had a talent. How could this be? Why is it that every one of these young women—and every one of us for that matter—has been blessed with inherent talents and abilities and yet we don't recognize them?

Why don't we know or share our talents?

I've found over the past fifteen years of coaching people about their talents that there are three **mindsets** that get in the way of talent discovery and manifestation:

1. The Deficit Perspective
2. The Scarcity Belief
3. The Humility Complex

Let's review each briefly.

DEFICIT PERSPECTIVE

We are trained and socialized from a very young age to figure out what's broken about us and fix it. We learn to focus on our deficiencies or weaknesses and work to improve those areas. This mindset is called the "deficit perspective." For example, if you think about employment, the last time you got an evaluation, what did you do? You probably skipped past the stuff you did well to get to that last page with all of the weaknesses on it. You then probably got hung up on that page wanting to focus on those weaknesses. Why? Because we want to fix it. We want to be "well-rounded."

Well-roundedness starts early in life when we enter school and explore many different subjects. Soon enough, report cards come out and our parents and teachers focus on where we're falling short. Not doing well in math? Time to ramp up the support. English grade dropping? Go all in on writing exercises and vocabulary quizzes. We claw and scratch and fight to get all A's, a sign that we are proficient and "well-rounded" across multiple subjects.

This mindset carries on into college, where we explore myriad core classes and electives, trying to be great at everything we do. We take on internships and participate in student activities to build a well-rounded resume or portfolio and fill in the gaps in our experience so that we are more appealing in the world of work.

We finally graduate and enter the world where we learn the great irony—the marketplace doesn't want well-rounded, and it certainly doesn't want people who are good at their weaknesses. The world wants specialists who are great at a few things. The world desperately needs people who are good at stuff.

I recently spoke to a group of parents and teachers about what's keeping our young people from identifying best-fit college majors and pursuing meaningful, aligned work. During the Q/A section at the end of the session, a teacher raised his hand and asked, "What is your philosophy on whether students should aim to become generalists who are good at lots of things or specialists who are expert at only a few?"

I couldn't figure out if he was baiting me, asking a rhetorical question, or sincerely wanted to know, but I said, "Let me put it this way. If I've got a sore tooth that's in desperate need of a root canal, I'm not interested in hiring Bobby the dentist who was average in dental school and only became a dentist because his mom and dad wanted him to become one. If I need to build a will to protect my assets, I don't want Sally who became a lawyer because she once watched *Law and Order* and it looked cool. If I've got a broken computer, I'm not hiring Carl the IT guy who majored in computer science because his math teacher told him he should. I'm hiring the specialist every time. I want the person who is an expert, who loves their craft, and who isn't great at everything but is a master at the thing I need."

We aren't meant to be generalists. Sure, we should attain a certain level of aptitude across many knowledge and skill domains, but never at the expense of our own uniqueness.

The deficit perspective says, "Sure, you're good at a few things, but you have so many more areas where you are deficient. Work on those and bring them up to par. Then you'll be happy." This perspective leaves us feeling like "there's someone else who could do this better" or "I'm not prepared enough." We've focused for so long on "what's left out" that we don't recognize the greatness that's in us—our unique, God-given ability that differentiates us from every other human on the planet.

By the way, this deficit perspective oftentimes manifests most when we speak to or teach others. We've got to be careful that every talk we give or lesson we teach isn't focused on identifying weaknesses and areas of deficit. "Sure, you're doing okay with charity, but your faith is weak and your hope is faltering. And you're praying a decent amount, but you really need to go to the temple more, read your scriptures for at least an hour a day, and bake a pie for every new family in the ward."

And where does this seem to manifest most heavily? Among the young people. Not so much with children, where we praise little Timmy's picture of Jesus or Sarah's singing in the children's program, but more so among the youth ages twelve to eighteen. I'm not sure why, but we tend to focus on deficits with this group—too much phone time, video games are bad, avoid gossip, and so on. Are these important topics? Absolutely. We should certainly prepare our kids for the time and trends in this generation. But we should also aim to balance this deficit focus with talking about what's great—talents and abilities, hope and faith, keys to prosperity and peace, and the good news of the gospel.

So what's at the root of the deficit perspective? Where does it come from? *Why* is our tendency to focus on what's left out? The answer lies in the way we are socialized, to be sure, but it's deeper than that. The root is actually fear.

Fear of what? Lots of things.

Sometimes we fear failure. What might happen if you claim to be talented at something and give it everything you have, only to fail? What would that say about your identity? It feels safer sometimes to focus on our weaknesses instead of magnifying our strengths. It's less risky. We might say, "If I fail at a weakness, oh well. It was a weakness, after all. But if I stick my neck out and try hard at a talent and it doesn't go well, I'm a failure."

Fear of failure can stop us from doing what we were meant to do for a really long time. In my coaching practice, I often help clients find joy in their work by first identifying their talents. These become their "competitive advantage." We then spend time planning for how to put those talents to work to get great results in their career. But inevitably, every coaching client approaches the same "cliff," and many get stuck on the precipice. The cliff is fear of failure, or the potential for them to invest in their talents, take the leap, and for it to not work out. The difference between those who succeed and those who pull back is their willingness to embrace the fear that comes with "raising their hand" and taking the leap *in spite of* the potential that it may fail. Fear of failure can lead to an overemphasis on our weaknesses.

Other times the deficit perspective creeps in because we fear the unknown. Having never used a talent publicly, we're not sure where it might lead. What if I'm not prepared for whatever comes from flexing that talent? This fear also masks itself as perfectionism. It sounds like, "I don't want to take the leap yet because I don't have everything ready or in place for whatever may come next." For example, when I wrote my first book it sat unpublished on my computer for seven years. Seven years! One day I was talking with a friend at work and he asked me why I hadn't published it.

"I don't have everything ready," I said.

"Ready for what?" he asked.

"Well, what if people want to know more, or what if they are looking for follow-up? What if they want to sign up for a program, or coaching, or additional assistance and I'm not ready?"

He smiled knowingly and said, "Then you'll figure it out. Cross that bridge when it comes. Just publish the book! Nobody's life is being changed as long as it sits on your hard drive."

How true. I wonder how often we hold back from volunteering to step up with the PTA at our kid's school, lead the music at church, or teach a course or workshop for our friends because we're not sure if we'll get it *exactly* right. And we're often more afraid of what else we might be asked to do if we're actually good at it! Fear of the unknown can halt progress toward growth. As my good friend often says, "There is no growth in the comfort zone, and there's no comfort in the growth zone." Change never feels great, and the unknown is full of all kinds of unexpected, but the growth we experience by leaning into the unknown and maximizing our talents far outweighs the regret that often comes from a life lived in comfort of holding back.

We also fear not being good enough, or not living up to expectations. What if I give it everything I have and it's still not enough?

In Doctrine and Covenants 60:2, the Lord told the Saints through Joseph Smith that He wasn't pleased with some because "they hide the talent which I have given unto them, because of the fear of man." Elder Ronald A. Rasband likewise said, "Sometimes we have a fear of using our talents. We use excuses such as 'I know I can't do that,' or 'Someone else can do it much better than I can,' or 'those listening to me, or watching me, will criticize and judge me.'"[2]

I can relate.

When I first returned home from my mission, I was highly motivated to find a best-fit career and start working toward it, but I felt stumped. I sought opinions from anyone who knew me well about where I might fit in the world of work. One mentor shared with me a common refrain: "Find something you love to do and you'll never work a day in your life." I thought about that and reflected on my mission. I loved to teach the gospel.

At the same time, I had been called as the Sunday School teacher for my BYU–Idaho student ward. I loved preparing lessons and thinking of unique and powerful ways to facilitate learning. One Sunday, in particular, stands out. It must have been parents weekend because I had a glut of mothers in the group. I prepared a great lesson on Joseph and the coat of many colors. I wore a rainbow-striped robe, and the lesson flowed really well. Afterward, two moms came up to me. One said that I should really consider a job teaching seminary for the LDS Church. The moment she said it I felt this rush of energy. It was the first time I had considered that I could get paid to do this every day. What a concept.

After that class it was settled. I'd be an early-morning seminary teacher.

I registered for the seminary pre-service class to learn to teach seminary for a living. I vividly remember showing up on the first day and seeing a room full of forty dynamic, energized, and well-equipped teachers. The pre-service trainer shared with us that only five of us would ever make it through the whole process. As I sat at the back of the room looking around, I felt totally discouraged. I had no confidence that I would be one of them. Several of these classmates seemed to already have inroads with the trainer and each other. I felt hopeless. I persisted through the class and met all of the requirements but bailed after one semester on the remainder of the program. I simply lacked the confidence. This is when I decided to get serious about a "real" major. I quit the program, put the seminary job in my rearview mirror, and changed my focus to a major in communications (and put myself on a trajectory for marketing Beano!). What stopped me? Likely the same thing that may be holding you back: what if I'm not good enough? What if I don't measure up? What if I don't meet expectations?

Fearing the response or reaction of others can stop us from doing things we might otherwise thrive at doing. The cruel irony is that we never invest in these talents for "fear of man," and they end up languishing within us and remaining undeveloped. All the while, the individuals we would most bless remain unserved. When we focus on our deficits in lieu of our talents, we do so at the expense of bettering humanity.

Little did I know at that time that I would later be called as an early-morning seminary teacher in my stake in Friendswood, Texas. Whether it was happenstance or not, the call came many years after I had begun to identify and invest in my talents in teaching and coaching and committed to use them for the benefit of God's kingdom. I gave everything I had to that calling and grew in my talent for teaching more than at any other time in my life. Interestingly, partway through the second year of teaching, the local seminary coordinator came to visit one of my classes. Afterward, he sat down with me to give me feedback on my class. I pulled out my notebook and prepared for the worst, assuming I had made some teaching errors. Instead, he looked at me and remarked, "You are a really gifted teacher. Have you ever considered doing this for a living?" I told him I had once considered it, many years before. He told me it was not too late and invited his area director to come down from Dallas to observe my teaching. This director did so, and I was eventually invited to be a part of the hiring pool for full-time seminary teachers. I didn't take the job, but the affirmation was rewarding. When we take the risk to put our talents to work, God can open doors.

Fear and faith cannot exist in the same sphere at the same time, and fear is a tool of the adversary to prevent us from learning our true identity. The deficit mindset is rooted in the fear that "I'm not good enough" or "I'm not talented in *that.*" It's the fear that you may not measure up, perform, and succeed.

Fear and the deficit mindset—left unchecked—will sabotage your development of talents.

SCARCITY BELIEF

I received this email a short time ago from a woman who had heard a podcast I did on talents and it hit me to the core:

> I just heard your interview. I know it was done a while ago, but I just found it and I really think it was life-changing for me. It made me feel free to claim my talents, and to see that I have had trouble with identifying them.
>
> As I listened, I remembered an experience when I was a child and I was upset because I didn't think I had any talents. I had two older brothers who were clearly talented. One was a budding artist and another clearly musically talented. Even my little sisters were starting to outshine me in 'every way.' All I could do was talk too much. I'd get sent to my room for talking too much at the dinner table.
>
> My siblings called me the "human tape recorder" because I would forget stories I'd already told and retell. My mom found me crying and asked what was wrong. I told her, "I don't have any talents!" She said, "You do have a talent. You care about people!" My only response was "That's not a talent." And I truly thought that if it is, everyone has it, everyone cares about people. But, as I listened to your conversation [on the podcast], the spirit reminded me of that experience and told me that I truly do have a talent of caring about people. I currently teach 1st grade and it is so easy for me to love those little people, even the kids who try to make life difficult for me. I also get a chance to talk and tell stories over and over again, which also truly is my talent. God gave me the talents that I need to make a difference in the world.
>
> Thank you for the message you are putting out there. It meant a lot to me!

Like this listener, you may sometimes feel like you don't have a talent. The Scarcity Belief is the concept that God had a certain number of talents to give out and only a few people got them. As in, to some He gave a bunch of talents, a smaller group got a few of the leftovers, and the rest of us were left out. Like, at some point in the premortal life when talents were being distributed, you stepped out of line to use the restroom and came back too late. "Sorry, all talents have been distributed. But you can still learn to be good at spreadsheets!"

We feel like talents are scarce and hard to find, and so if we can't readily identify any then we must not have them. This leaves us thinking, "There's not enough talent going around."

Why would that be?

Why would God, who is all-powerful and omniscient, reserve talents for the select few?

We learn in Doctrine and Covenants 46:11-12 that "to every man (and woman) is given a gift by the Spirit of God. To some is given one, and to some is given another."

Everyone has one! You weren't left out.

This scarcity belief is dangerous, because it leaves you to believe there are only a few talented people and the rest of us are doomed to develop our skills through grit.

This is especially true when we look at those we admire and respect. We see the end product of years of developing talent and assume their greatness is a product of their calling or ordination. What we don't see is that their current awesomeness is really the manifestation of years of identifying and developing talent into true strength and using it for the benefit of humankind.

Thus, there's enough talent to go around.

Elder Marvin J. Ashton of the Quorum of the Twelve Apostles said this:

> One of the great tragedies of life, it seems to me, is when a person classifies himself as someone who has no talents or gifts. When, in disgust or discouragement, we allow ourselves to reach depressive levels of despair because of our demeaning

> self-appraisal, it is a sad day for us and a sad day in the eyes of God. For us to conclude that we have no gifts when we judge ourselves by stature, intelligence, grade-point average, wealth, power, position, or external appearance is not only unfair but unreasonable. . . .
>
> God has given each of us one or more special talents. . . . It is up to each of us to search for and build upon the gifts which God has given. We must remember that each of us is made in the image of God, that there are no unimportant persons. Everyone matters to God and to his fellowmen."[3]

There is no talent shortage. The scarcity belief is a myth. It's a trap! Don't fall into it. Further, don't let yourself use this as an excuse not to discover and use your talents.

I could easily see somebody saying, "Sure, I might have talents, but there are probably lots of other people with the same talents who are way better (deficit mindset), so I should just not bother." It's important to note that each person has unique talents and a unique way of using them. And a unique combination of talents that work together in powerful ways. As Paul counseled Timothy in 1 Timothy 4:14, "Neglect not the gift that is in thee."

THE HUMILITY COMPLEX

Another thing that gets in the way of recognizing talents is humility. Wait, what? That's sacrilegious. Humility, the very essence of our religion, a trait that is requisite for entrance into the kingdom of God, might actually be the thing preventing us from identifying our talents?

Let me explain.

I remember a moment in college when I was tasked with creating a presentation for a public relations class. The day before it was due, I had an idea crystallize about how I would present the topic. I put together a slide deck and showed up on the day of the class, pumped and ready.

When it was my turn, I stood and presented with everything I had. It felt easy and natural. I felt smooth. In fact, it didn't really feel like it was all that hard.

Afterward, a classmate approached and complimented me on the presentation, saying it was one of the best they had seen. I immediately felt insecure. Really? One of the best? But I didn't even spend that much time on it.

Immediately I said, "Aw thanks, but it was nothing. I didn't even work that hard on it."

She replied, "Really? Because I was tweaking mine all week and feel like it just fell flat."

All week? I felt even more self-conscious. I threw this thing together with a stroke of inspiration and it was the best thing ever? And she worked all week for something she felt was average?

I call this the "aw shucks" syndrome, or the tendency to wave off a compliment that might otherwise tell us something powerful about our talents, simply because of our desire to be perceived as humble. But we are socialized to believe humility is synonymous with self-deprecation. Said another way, if we didn't work that hard at it, it must not be a talent. Ironically, the very essence of talents is that they are fluid, easy, and natural. We don't *have* to work all that hard at them because they are innate!

We as a society overvalue humility. Think about the last time you did something well. When people approach you to laud praise and compliments on you, what's your natural reaction? "Aw, c'mon. It wasn't that good. The message is really the powerful thing. And the audience was great. Anybody could have done it."

The trouble here is that over time we actually begin to believe what we are saying. When we "aw shucks" a compliment long enough, we begin to convince ourselves that what we did wasn't really all that great.

What might be a better response? Maybe, "Thank you! I appreciate that!" The key to accepting clues from others about our talents without engaging in pride is knowing from whence those talents come. One commenter on the podcast I gave said this:

> I think lots of people are trying to avoid the appearance of pride (or actual pride!) when they deny talents. It just feels too prideful to acknowledge a talent. My favorite scripture in connection with that

> is Alma 26:11–12: "But Ammon said unto him: I do not boast in my own strength, nor in my own wisdom; but behold, my joy is full, yea, my heart is brim with joy, and I will rejoice in my God. Yea, I know that I am nothing; as to my strength I am weak; therefore I will not boast of myself, but I will boast of my God, for in his strength I can do all things; yea, behold, many mighty miracles we have wrought in this land, for which we will praise his name forever." When we thank others for recognizing the talents God gave us, and acknowledge all good gifts are from him, we are in no danger of pride.

My worry is that we get so used to waving off a compliment or not inhaling the praise that we eventually talk ourselves out of the very things we do best. If you consistently say, "Aw, it was nothing, really. I'm not even sure I'm that good at it," you may eventually begin to believe that.

Let me be clear—the biggest room in the world is the room for improvement. You can always find ways to improve and grow. You also need to work at growing and developing your talents. There are certainly tens of thousands of people who are better writers, speakers, trainers, coaches, and leaders than I am, and developing my talents is a lifelong quest. That said, you can acknowledge a talent without being overly prideful. When you get a compliment, just say thank you, and internally acknowledge it as a God-given talent that you are constantly working to develop and improve. More important, take note of that data point. When someone objectively tells you that you are better than average at something, that could be a clue about your talents.

It's a "both/and," not an "either/or." You can be both humble *and* self-aware, not either humble *or* self-aware.

Aside from these three **mindsets,** one other thing gets in the way of people developing and maximizing their talents: procrastination. Let's address it here briefly, and I'll touch on it again at the end of the book with specific steps you can take to develop your talents.

PROCRASTINATION

Oliver Wendell Holmes Sr. said: "Many people die with their music still in them. Why is this so? Too often it is because they are always getting ready to live. Before they know it, time runs out."[4]

The poet Rabindranath Tagore similarly said, "I have spent my days stringing and unstringing my instrument, while the song I came to sing remains unsung."[5]

I wonder how often procrastination prevents us from exercising the gifts and talents with which the Lord has blessed us. My guess would be way too often. There's always something else "worthwhile" you can find to do, like housework or grocery shopping. Or fixing the rain gutters.

This one frequently manifests as a shortage of time, as if some of us have more hours in the day than others. "If I only had more time, I would develop and use that talent." Last I checked, everyone gets twenty-four hours each day. The difference is in how we choose to use them. God has made clear how He expects us to use the time we have here on earth. Elder Henry D. Taylor of the Quorum of the Seventy gave this analysis in his talk "Gifts and Talents":

> When we receive a gift or talent from the Lord, we have an obligation to use it. In a parable the Savior told of a man who was preparing to go to a far country. Before leaving he entrusted to one servant five talents, to another two talents, and to another one talent. The first two servants invested their talents and doubled them. The last servant fearfully buried his one talent in the earth. Upon returning, the traveler said to each of the first two servants, "Well done, thou good and faithful servant," but to the servant who had buried his talent he said:
>
> "Thou wicked and slothful servant, thou knewest that I reap where I sowed not, and gather where I have not strawed:
>
> "Thou oughtest therefore to have put my money to the exchangers, and then at my coming I should have received mine own money with usury.
>
> "Take therefore the talent from him, and give it unto him which hath ten talents.
>
> "And cast ye the unprofitable servant into outer darkness: there shall be weeping and gnashing of teeth." (Matthew 25:26–28, 20[6]

Notice the word "obligation" as in a duty or commitment; something to which we are legally or morally bound. We shouldn't just use our talents because God gave them to us. We should use them because we are obligated to do so, bound by commitments we've made to God to consecrate our talents to the building up of His kingdom. And, if we choose instead to bury these gifts, that which we have could be taken from us and given to someone more willing to do what Father asks. Now, I've never been a fan of motivating people through fear—and weeping and gnashing of teeth in outer darkness sounds scary enough—but it's important to recognize that not using your talents isn't just a "you" thing, it's an "us" thing. You don't only hurt yourself, we—the world—miss out on what you have to offer. Don't delay! Discover your gifts and put them to work every day in every situation. Not using these gifts puts these "superpowers" in the same category as that ab-cruncher you got for Christmas from Uncle Lou or that llama-wool sweater you got for your birthday from Aunt Sally. And these gifts are certainly more valuable than those.

Your family needs it, your employer needs it, and the world definitely needs what you have to give.

In his 2002 talk, "I Believe I Can, I Knew I Could," President James E. Faust said,

> Some of us are too content with what we may already be doing. We stand back in the 'eat, drink, and be merry' mode when opportunities for growth and development abound. We miss opportunities to build up the kingdom of God because we have the passive notion that someone else will take care of it. The Lord tells us that He will give more to those who are willing. They will be magnified in their efforts, like the little blue engine as it pulled the train up the mountain. But to those who say, "We have enough, from them shall be taken away even that which they have."[7]

There is no greater time than the present to invest in discovering and maximizing what you do best. Planning doesn't make you better at what you do. Practice does! Don't wait to develop your talent, punting your growth to some future day. And don't assume that your offering is too small or insignificant. Remember: all those who grow their talents "experience the joy of the Lord"—whether they have two talents, five, or more. Try, fail, refine, and try again.

THE WAY OUT

So how do you escape these three **mindsets** and the allure of procrastination? As with most fears, self-doubts, and challenges in mortality, the solution to emerge is relatively straightforward. Notice that I didn't say "simple," because there is nothing easy about it. But the way out is clearly defined. It starts with understanding your identity. Get clear about who you really are, and then learn to believe and accept that.

As quoted at the beginning of the book, President Spencer W. Kimball taught that "Jesus knew who he was and why he was here on this planet. That meant he could lead from strength rather than from uncertainty or weakness."[8]

Understand the origin of your talents is the precursor to identifying them.

NOTES

1. James E. Faust, "I Believe I Can, I Knew I Could," October 2002 general conference, churchofjesuschrist.org/study/general-conference/2002/10/i-believe-i-can-i-knew-i-could?lang=eng.
2. Ronald A. Rasband, "You've Got Talent." *New Era*, July 2018, churchofjesuschrist.org/study/new-era/2018/07/youve-got-talent?lang=eng.
3. Marvin J. Ashton, "There Are Many Gifts." *Ensign*, Nov. 1987, churchofjesuschrist.org/study/general-conference/1987/10/there-are-many-gifts?lang=eng
4. The Voiceless; reported in Bartlett's Familiar Quotations, 10th ed. (1919).
5. W. Radice, *Selected poems of Rabindranath Tagore*, (Penguin Classics, 2005).
6. Henry D. Taylor, "Gifts and Talents." *New Era*, Aug. 1977, churchofjesuschrist.org/study/new-era/1977/08/gifts-and-talents?lang=eng.
7. James E. Faust, "I Believe I Can, I Knew I Could." *Ensign*, Nov. 2002, churchofjesuschrist.org/study/general-conference/2002/10/i-believe-i-can-i-knew-i-could?lang=eng.
8. Spencer W. Kimball, "Jesus, The Perfect Leader." *Ensign*, Aug. 1979, churchofjesuschrist.org/study/ensign/1979/08/jesus-the-perfect-leader?lang=eng.

CHAPTER 3

The Origin of Talent

"When we rejoice in beautiful scenery, great art, and great music, it is but the flexing of instincts acquired in another place and another time."[1]

—NEAL A. MAXWELL

I want to take you back. Way back. To a time that neither you nor I remember before we were ever born. I'm talking about the premortal world, where we first developed the talents that we would eventually bring with us to this earth life. Do you remember? Neither do I. Gratefully, prophets have shared insights and glimpses into that time to give us an idea of what happened in the premortal world.

What do we know about the premortal world? We learn from Doctrine and Covenants 138:56 that "even before they were born, they, with many others, received their first lessons in the world of spirits and were prepared to come forth in the due time of the Lord to labor in his vineyard for the salvation of the souls of men." This verse alone says quite a lot. First, before we were born we received lessons. We were taught, instructed by heavenly teachers. I don't remember the lessons I was taught, but I imagine part of that learning process included development of talents and abilities. Effective education always utilizes principles of experience and application, of practice and growth. We learn that we lived in a world full of spirits, the sons and daughters of God. We also learn that we were prepared for the purpose of coming to earth to labor for the salvation of the "souls of men," or the salvation of our brothers and sisters. Again, I imagine the talents we bring with us help to facilitate that earthly mission.

Elder Bruce R. McConkie of the Quorum of the Twelve Apostles taught this amazing concept:

> All the spirits of men, while yet in the Eternal Presence, developed aptitudes, talents, capacities, and abilities of every sort, kind, and degree. During the long expanse of life which then was, an infinite variety of talents and abilities came into being. As the ages rolled, no two spirits remained alike. Mozart became a musician; Einstein centered his interest in mathematics; Michelangelo turned his attention to painting. . . . Abraham and Moses and all of the prophets sought and obtained the talent for spirituality. . . .
>
> When we pass from preexistence to mortality, we bring with us the traits and talents there developed. True, we forget what went before because we are here being tested, but the capacities and abilities that then were ours are yet resident within us. Mozart is still a musician; Einstein retains his mathematical abilities; Michelangelo his artistic talent; Abraham, Moses, and the prophets their spiritual talents and abilities. . . . And all men with their infinitely varied talents and personalities pick up the course of progression where they left it off when they left the heavenly realms.[2]

Our uniqueness, our differences, are what make us strong. The diversity of talents that God gave to His children require that we work together—and for each other—like a giant tapestry of talents to help save the souls of men. The teacher has to teach, the builder must construct, the artist must inspire, and the chemist must discover. We all work together to contribute our piece to the advancing of knowledge and the growth of humankind.

As a Seventy in the Church, Elder McConkie shared this additional insight: "In this prior life, this premortal existence, this preexistence, we developed various capacities and talents. Some developed them in one field and some in another. The most important of all fields was the field of spirituality—the ability, the talent, the capacity to recognize truth."[3]

Think of it! *All the spirits of men and women.* Again, not some of us. Not one of us. ALL.

Before you and I came to earth, we developed the seeds of talents. We strengthened aptitudes and abilities, and none were necessarily the same. Some became expert in one thing and some in another. For a wise purpose known to God, we forgot these talents and aptitudes when were born on earth. But we weren't left without clues. We have certain interests and passions that draw us in. We are given clues from the Holy Ghost when we do things we are naturally adept at. We stumble upon activities that light our fire and make us feel strong, in control, natural, powerful, and inspired. And yet, we don't all get there. Some discover their uniqueness while others struggle to find it.

This begs the question, so why is Mozart *Mozart*? Or what made Einstein *Einstein?* I believe the answer is that they *intentionally* discovered, nurtured, practiced, developed, and maximized their innate abilities. They were perceptive enough to identify and draw out those innate abilities, and then go "all in" on them.

In fact, Mozart was able to play the piano by age three. His father and sister were both talented musicians as well, so he was raised in an environment that encouraged development of his talents. I also think it is worth noting that he began to develop his skills before he had the capacity to evaluate whether they were "good" or not. Meaning, a three-year-old can match pitch, but is often more interested in his work of play than creating an earth-shattering composition.

On the other hand, when Einstein was a kid, he was called "the dopey one." He was a late speaker and socially awkward. He's a good example of someone whose talents were not obvious to other people, but who just steadfastly followed curiosity where it led. He pursued his talents, developed them, and made significant contributions to the world, in spite of the challenges he experienced.

Interestingly, Einstein, who was himself a violinist, once said this of Mozart: "Mozart's music is so pure and beautiful that I see it as a reflection of the inner beauty of the universe itself."[4]

Everybody is given talent seeds in the premortal world. Maybe that's why some music resonates with people so universally. It explains something we all long to understand about the universe and our place in it. It feels true. And I think talents are like that. They feel true.

This thought brings me hope that each of us can be a "Mozart" of our craft, an "Einstein" in our ability if we can get clear about what makes us unique and grow it.

Elder Joseph Fielding Smith, then of the Quorum of the Twelve Apostles, said "During the ages in which we dwelt in the premortal state we not only developed our various characteristics and showed our worthiness and ability, or the lack of it, but we were also where such progress could be observed."[5]

I assume we had divine tutors who taught and trained us in the innate talents we possessed. Some progressed further in their talent development, but we all bring those talents—in whatever form they're in—into this life, with the charge to maximize them.

Likewise, Elder L. Tom Perry of the Quorum of the Twelve Apostles said, "In the premortal world we were taught the Father's plan of redemption and enjoyed moral agency. Through the use of this agency, men and women developed varying appetites, talents, and capacities over time and no spirits remained the same."[6]

You came to earth pre-packaged with innate abilities. Many "enemies of talent" stand in the way of discovering those abilities and clarifying your true identity, but with concerted effort you can discover your talents and grow them.

In fact, you were born into your present family and circumstances for the intentional purpose of developing the aptitudes you began to develop in the premortal realm. President Joseph F. Smith said, "He has chosen the time and place for each of us to be born so we can learn the lessons we personally need and do the most good with our individual talents and personalities."[7]

Over the past fifteen years, I've invested significant time in helping thousands of people identify and grow their talents in the spirit of leading with more power, finding a more gratifying career, serving more effectively in their calling, and leading more intentionally in their families. Developing your talents is really a process of discovering what is innately a part of your makeup as a spiritual son or daughter of Heavenly Parents.

In the next chapters, I'd like to share the process and approach I use time and time again to empower people to identify and use their talents in the service of God. I encourage you to have a pen and paper or journal handy and read the next chapters with a spirit of introspection. Ultimately, the Father of us all is the greatest source of knowledge regarding who you were in the preexistent state, who you are today, and who He hopes you will become. Listen to your inner voice!

NOTES

1. Neal A. Maxwell, "The Great Plan of the Eternal God," *Ensign*, May 1984, 21.
2. "Recognizing and Developing Talents and Abilities," *The Gospel and the Productive Life Student Manual Religion 150*, chapter 7, 46, churchofjesuschrist.org/study/manual/the-gospel-and-the-productive-life-student-manual/chapter-7?lang=eng.
3. "Our Premortal Life," *Doctrines of the Gospel Student Manual*, chapter 6, churchofjesuschrist.org/study/manual/doctrines-of-the-gospel-student-manual/6-premortal-life?lang=eng.
4. W. Isaacson, *Einstein: His life and universe* (Simon & Schuster, 2007).
5. Joseph Fielding Smith, *Doctrines of Salvation*, 1:57.
6. L. Tom Perry, "Give Heed unto the Word of the Lord." [CES fireside for young adults, May 2, 1999], 2).
7. "Spirit Children of Heavenly Parents," Gospel Topics, Churchofjesuschrist.org.

CHAPTER 4

Identifying Talents

"I would like to be remembered as someone who did the best she could with the talent she had."[1]

—J. K. ROWLING

Clear your mind.

No really, I want you to play along with an exercise I use with clients every day.

If your mind is clear, then I want you to think of a moment when you were at your best. One of your "best days ever." But let me add a few caveats:

1. I'm not interested in a day when you didn't have anything to do so you slept in, lounged around, and added little value. Although those days are great, they won't serve our purpose.
2. I'm not interested in a moment when someone else achieved something great, like your daughter's wedding, your best friend's graduation, or the day when Junior finally hit the ball.

I want you to hone in on a moment or day when you personally were at your best and you added value to the world around you. A day when you contributed something and felt successful afterward. Think of a moment when you were at your very best—when you felt fluid and natural.

Do you have it locked in? Now reflect on that moment using these questions:

- Who was there? Who were you serving or doing that thing to or for?
- What were you doing? Specifically, what was it that made you feel strong?
- Why was it powerful? Of all the moments that could have come to your mind, why that one?

Let me take a stab at answering that last question: You felt what you did in that moment and on that day is because **you were using a talent.**

In workshops, I'll have people describe that moment in detail to the person sitting next to them. Invariably, they become animated, energized, and demonstrative, using their hands to rehash the day.

I'll ask the audience to give me some words to describe how that day felt, and to tell me if they feel that same energy again now. The words are always similar:

- Authentic
- Powerful
- In control
- Confident
- Natural
- Comfortable

Then we'll pull back the curtain. *Why* did you feel that way? How is that all of us could have a different best day ever, and yet the resulting feelings were the same: power, strength, confidence, inspiration? The reason? Talent. You felt the way you did on that day because you were using a talent. Talents release energy, and they're what makes it your best day ever.

So what, then, is a talent? Talents are things you do naturally, consistently well. Think *energy.* Because they are natural, fluid, and easy, talents release energy. What is energy? It's that rush of endorphins that confirms that you did something effectively and that leaves you feeling strong, confident, and in the zone.

Energy is the hallmark of talent. Or, better yet, it's the byproduct.

Talents are developed at a very young age and manifest as highways in our brains across which impulses travel. Because these pathways are large and developed, the transmissions flow easily, releasing a feeling of fluidity and associated endorphins into our systems. These endorphins then manifest as energy boosts that make us want to do more of whatever we were doing. We feel strong.

Energy may also be the word the world uses to describe the manifestation of the Spirit. Remember the two disciples on the road to Emmaus: "Did not our heart burn within us, while he talked with us by the way, and while he opened to us the scriptures?" (Luke 24:32). Energy feels like the warm, reinforcing comfort of the Spirit prompting us to keep doing what we're doing.

Perhaps this energy we feel when utilizing our God-given talents and abilities—this affirming fluidity and reinforcement—is a manifestation of the Holy Ghost, reinforcing in us what was inherent to us in the premortal world. Regardless of whether "energy" is, the Holy Ghost or simply our hard-wired brains signaling the use of wide-open neural pathways, the result is key. Talents are directly linked to feelings and emotion, meaning that the easiest way to identify them is to reflect on moments when we felt the hallmark feelings of talent.

When I worked through this exercise with Lindsay, she had an "a-ha" moment about the path she was on. Lindsay works as an IT auditor for a major multinational organization, but you'd never guess that if you met her at a party or social gathering. She's empathic, emotional, intelligent, outgoing, bright, good-natured, and keenly interested in every person she meets. She makes people feel like the most important person in the room. Based on this, you might peg her for a teacher, educator, counselor, or other people-facing professional.

Lindsay was at a crossroads when we met, trying to make a decision about her future career path. Based on my knowledge about

Lindsay, I knew she was a prolific dancer, a great cook, and a creative person. I couldn't wait to hear how those things intersected with . . . auditing IT systems for multinational organizations. As it turns out, what I was missing was clarity about her true talents.

I asked Lindsay right off the bat to describe the parts of her job that give her *energy.* She lit up and rattled off the following things (read: clues about her talents):

- I'm organized.
- I love to gather data to understand systems.
- I'm good at finding people's problems, diagnosing them, and figuring out solutions to solve them.
- I enjoy training new hires, teaching, and onboarding people—being the expert!
- I like to help people make sense of systems.

Note the use of words like "I love" or "I enjoy" or "I'm good at." When I hear these words, I perk up. On the other side of these phrases are almost always clues about talent. Why? Remember, talents are things that we enjoy, that feel fluid, natural, easy, and motivating. They are the things we are drawn to do over and over. Other people often recognize and praise us for them and we "can't help but" raise our hand to them over and over again.

Looking at this short list, Lindsay may not have felt like these words and phrases were special. But to me, they are gold. I meet with dozens of people a week and have seen the uniqueness in each and every individual. People are so different, and the combination of the top three to five talents that separate most individuals from the rest of us is always special. In fact, a commonality among most people is that they think what they do isn't all that different from what everyone else does. "Isn't everyone organized?" or "Doesn't everyone love to be the expert and train or teach new hires?" No! Not necessarily. These things make you unique.

I pressed on with Lindsay and asked about times in her life when she was at her best. I asked her to share with me what other people have noticed about her talents. I also asked her to reflect on what gifts she thinks God has blessed her with. Finally, I asked the golden question: what's the intersection between your love for dance and your aptitude for IT systems work? This was the "ah-a" moment for both of us.

She said, "What I love about dance isn't so much the fluidity of it or the movement. What I love is that dance is **governed by technical rules and procedures**. In dance, I need to **take a lot of information and synthesize it** into a meaningful routine. I love **teaching people how to dance because I have expertise to share**, and I like **the problem-solving aspect of figuring out how to convey a mood or emotion** through a dance routine. I **excel when things are black and white** and **love to perform**."

Wow. Do you see it? Talents are so transferable that they pop in every activity we do. No wonder she likes IT auditing. She's putting the same talents to work, just in a different environment. I asked Lindsay if she had considered any other professions. She said counseling or maybe personal finance, because "I'm very **analytical**. I like to **learn about people's problems, diagnose them, and help them find solutions**. I'm **organized and systematic** in helping people **work through their problems** and get energy from **adding value to people's lives**." What's more, she said family and friends have always told her she's good at these things and she's felt drawn to them in her own time, reading about personality types, emotional intelligence, personal finance, and helping people increase their awareness! Outside perspectives and feedback are a great data point to help narrow down talent.

So, what's the solution for Lindsay? What type of job should she pursue? The reality is that it doesn't matter, as long as she finds something that puts her talents front and center. Jobs or careers don't make us happy. Chores and volunteer activities often don't either. In fact, many people reading this book may say that their Church calling doesn't necessarily drive their joy. I would say that's because these things aren't meant to drive joy in and of themselves. Chores, jobs, volunteer activities, callings, and even raising children are the "what" that we do, but talents are the "how." Talents are the approach we take that makes our imprint on the work special, unique, and powerful. Joy comes from putting your talents to work regardless of the situation or environment. Find a way to use your talents each day and you will unlock the feelings associated with talent: energy, happiness, fluidity, and joy.

DOING WHAT YOU LOVE

Talents are the key to doing what you love—and loving what you do. People often share the idea that you should "just do what you love." This is both right and wrong. Yes, you should pursue something you love because you are more invested in things you love and you get more return on your investment. Think puppies. Or your family. But they may be wrong in suggesting that if you love singing you should be a singer. Or if you love basketball you should head for the NBA.

I made the mistake of charting a course to a career in professional basketball that ended when I was fourteen and got cut in tryouts. I didn't get far. All my life when people suggested I should just do what I love for a living I poopooed them, feeling like I had missed my calling in basketball and was forever doomed to just work out the rest of my days in job purgatory. "Well, if I failed at doing what I love, I guess I should fall back into line with the day laborers." Then, one day in 2008, I had a revelation that changed the way I pursue what I love to do: When you ask yourself, "Well, what do I love to do?" I think you are asking the wrong question. Instead, try asking, "What do I love about what I love to do?" Say what? Here's what I mean: I love basketball, and yet I can't do that for a career. But one day seven years ago I looked at it differently and instead asked, "What do I love about basketball?" Through some serious guided reflection, I came up with this list:

- Working with a group toward a common goal (winning) versus working alone.
- The strategy of working in a dynamic (constantly changing) environment to achieve a goal.
- The communication that takes place on the court, both verbal and nonverbal.
- The instant gratification of scoring versus delayed reward.

- The use of intuition to see the court and envision how it could shift in the next few seconds.
- The competitiveness, winning, and the affirmation that comes with winning.
- Finding connections between teammates during the game that result in success—that whole synergy thing.
- Being better than other people at the same activity.
- Encouraging others and motivating them to be better.

The concept is clear. Basketball isn't what I really love. The act of putting an orange ball through an orange rim doesn't yield energy in and of itself. It's the other elements of the activity that drive the energy and joy. When I looked at what I loved about basketball and what I love about my current job it's the same. Here's how it fits:

- Working with a group—working with a team to create leadership programming for individuals.
- Strategy in an ever-changing, dynamic environment—predicting the needs of my target audience (a dynamic audience) and strategizing to be most effective.
- Communication—training, teaching, and coaching one-on-one.
- Instant gratification—watching over the course of a thirty-minute session as someone "gets it."
- Connectedness—finding connections between seemingly disparate ideas to help a client discover their leadership style or career path.
- Envisioning future trends—creating a three-to-five-year vision for the organization.
- Competitiveness—being better at my job than I was last year.
- Affirmation—clients thanking me for helping them change their lives.

This was mind-blowing to me, and I haven't looked at what I love to do the same ever since. I don't generally love things for the sake of loving them; I love them because of what they allow me to do. Basketball is the manifestation of my talent and passion, not the talent and passion itself.

Doing what you love is not a "do-or-die" proposition. If you love to sing, you don't have to be a professional singer, and if you love numbers, you're not destined to be an accountant. Anyone can do what they love most of the time if they look at what they love and ask what they love about it and then do more of that wherever they are. Identify the transferables and transfer them to every activity you do. If I do any of the above bullets as a husband or father or Sunday School teacher or t-ball coach, I feel the same satisfaction as if I were on the court dunking on someone's head or working my job. It's a powerful principle.

Thinking back to the "best day ever" activity, your best days are often those days when you were putting your talents to work. Depending on how frequently you utilize talents, some of you may have many "best moment" experiences where others may have relatively few. But no one will be devoid of experiences when their talents were utilized. Remember: each of us has talents, and every one of us has opportunities to use them. The great paradox of talent is that because it is natural to us it is also difficult to identify. So let's talk more specifically about how to identify talent.

TALENT IDENTIFICATION TECHNIQUES

Talents are raw material and the building blocks of strengths and success. They can be developed and we can gain more. The Lord said in Doctrine and Covenants 82:18, "And all this for the benefit of the church of the living God, that every man may improve upon his talent, that every man may gain other talents, yea, even an hundred fold, to be cast into the Lord's storehouse, to become the common property of the whole church." Remember, every one of us is given talents for the purpose of benefiting others. "To some is given one, and to some is given another, that all may be profited thereby" (D&C 46:11–12).

Talents come in many varieties, but often fall into one of three categories:

1. Thinking talents are the way you gather, process, and make decisions with information and mental images. These might include:
    - Making connections between seemingly disparate pieces of information
    - Arranging and cataloging information
    - Learning and remembering information
    - Analyzing information
    - Strategizing
2. Feeling talents include the way to connect with people, emotion, or your senses:
    - Relating easily with others
    - Influencing the mood in the room
    - Empathizing easily with others
    - Identifying and maximizing individual needs
    - Being inclusive and helping everyone feel like they belong
    - Meeting new people and gaining their trust
    - Doing talents include the way you go about getting things done:
    - Motivating a group of people to accomplish a task
    - Creating and executing a plan of action
    - Focusing on an objective to get stuff done
    - Making something better than it was before you got to it

3. Doing talents are the most easily recognizable because we can observe them. Think of the talented organizer, speaker, coach, dancer, athlete, or musician. In fact, any time that I ask groups of people about talents, they almost always *only* focus on doing talents. A few years back, I spoke to a youth class about talents and asked them to make a list with me of talents. They said:

- Dancing
- Singing
- Sports
- Music
- Karate
- Throwing axes (this is about where the list began to devolve)

Notice that most people think "observable actions" actions when identifying talents. Adults make much the same list, replacing "throwing axes" with something more benign like "cooking" or "public speaking." However, thinking and feeling talents are just as legitimate although they can be difficult to identify. I had a young woman tell me that she's always been good at listening to others and helping them feel "heard" but never realized that was a talent. I asked her what she thought it was. "I'm not sure," she said. "I guess I just thought everyone does that." Not so! At least not in the unique way that she does it.

We all have many talents and they likely span all three groupings: thinking, feeling, and doing. Of course, not all talents fall neatly into these categories, so don't be discouraged by trying to sort your talents. These categories may simply help you home in on potential areas of talent.

In reality, talents are as varied and diverse as the people who possess them. Below are some additional examples:

TALENTS THAT ARE EASY TO RECOGNIZE

- Being a good athlete
- Intelligence, being good at school
- Gardening
- Singing
- Dancing
- Playing a musical instrument
- Drawing, painting, sculpting
- Cooking, baking
- Writing

- Public speaking
- Teaching
- Acting
- Composing songs
- Having a good sense of humor
- Sewing
- Being a good photographer
- Storytelling
- Repairing things

TALENTS THAT ARE NOT AS EASY TO NOTICE

- Having empathy
- Being a peacemaker
- Being positive and energetic
- Communicating effectively
- Being a good listener
- Having self-control, discipline
- Being able to make decisions
- Setting goals, getting tasks accomplished
- Being good with children
- Giving service
- Inputting or retaining information
- Mentally organizing information
- Analyzing and sorting data
- Being friendly and kind to others
- Being able to make people feel comfortable and at ease with you
- Seeing the good in others
- Thrift, good at saving money
- Punctuality

Talents are also more nuanced and transferable than simply "ice skating" or "cooking." In fact, I often suggest that those aren't in and of themselves talents but rather "manifestations" of talent. Let me explain.

Talents are the raw building blocks of what we do well. I once explained to a group of teachers that teaching isn't actually a talent; it's the manifestation of a talent. After the booing quieted down, I explained that teaching is really the convergence of several talents at play, such as the following:

- The ability to create a plan to lead to an outcome.
- The talent for self-expression.
- Intuition, or the ability to sense the needs of others.
- The ability to read the room.
- A knack for strategically approaching a topic in a way that engages.
- The talent for driving toward a specific goal and achieving it in a short time frame.
- Any many more!

In other words, five "talented" teachers could each be great for a totally different reason. The difference between each of them—their uniqueness—is their talent.

Likewise, musicians are talented because they can blow a trumpet well or have fast-moving fingers. Those are skills that come from practice. Their talent, though, might be retaining concepts or memorization or even seeing the big picture that ties the smaller notes together. Maybe they are talented at conveying emotion. The music ends up as the manifestation, but the talent is much deeper and rawer.

This also means that those talents are transferable, as we saw in Lindsay's story. That teacher could take their talent for "organizing various pieces to achieve an outcome" and apply it to decorating, cooking, or planning a family activity. The musician could take their knack for seeing the big picture and how notes tie together and apply it to creating an emergency preparedness plan for the ward. Talents are the raw material that manifests in different ways.

Thus, when someone tells me they are talented at rock climbing or music, I don't doubt them, but deep down I wonder what raw ability drives that activity. What's the true talent? I think there is power in boiling down talent to its most basic—and transferable—form.

The scriptures abound with talented people who deployed their innate abilities in different ways to achieve a desired outcome. Nephi comes to mind for me. After reviewing the life of Nephi, one could say he had the "feeling" talents of patience, long-suffering, forgiveness, or resilience. He used these talents with his brothers, his parents, wicked King Laban, and in the promised land with his people. He suffered in the wilderness, on a ship, and in the promised land, but pressed forward diligently. He was also gifted at "doing" talents such as engineering things with his hands. He made a bow, built a ship, and taught his people to be industrious, constructing weapons of war, tools, and even a temple. He was a gifted writer, scribing the powerful, poetic psalm in 2 Nephi 4. He likely possessed the "thinking" talent of being reflective, retreating often to pray to the Lord, pondering the scriptures, and processing what was happening around him. This talent led him to see the vision of the tree of life that his father saw, talk with an angel on a mountaintop about the birth of Christ and the unfolding of the history of the world, and generate ideas for constructing tools to build a ship. Nephi was talented! And he combined those talents with effort and the help of the Lord to do amazing things. Take note that the ultimate execution of those talents was heavily dependent on the Lord's hand, but the raw ability was inborn in him. Discovering and magnifying our talents in combination with obedience and the power of God makes for a powerful formula for accomplishing miraculous things.

Discovering talents can not only be empowering, but it can also give us a sense of direction and purpose, and a "tool belt" of strength to pull from to thrive in the trials and challenges placed before us. In order to help my clients identify their talents, I use two activities: feedback and reflection. I'll discuss them here briefly.

ACTIVITY 1: FEEDBACK FROM OUTSIDE THE FRAME

What makes the *Mona Lisa* so interesting? I have no idea, but I'm also not an art aficionado.

However, many other people do know what makes her so interesting, and they travel across the globe to see her.

She's amazing.

Here's the thing: she doesn't know she's amazing.

She sits in her frame looking out at the people walking by and wonders, "Why do these people stop and stare? What do they see? Is there something behind me? What's so interesting?"

She doesn't get it. She doesn't know how awesome she is because of this important principle: it's hard to see the picture when you're in the frame.

Likewise, you might have little-to-no idea what your talents are, but other people do. If I gathered twenty of your closest friends, family, and colleagues into a room and asked them what makes you great, they'd probably identify five to ten consistent things that make you uniquely you.

But you can't see it.

Herein lies the great paradox of talent: the only person who doesn't seem to know what you do best is YOU. Why? Because talents are natural, innate, and fluid. These talents are so much a part of who you are that you don't work to deploy them. They express naturally in your life and work.

Imagine figuring out these talents, then using them to guide the way you work and serve. What if you could identify what you do best and use that as the foundation for your career, calling, or leadership? Better yet, don't imagine, go do it.

How?

To carry the analogy further, how would Mona Lisa recognize her beauty? Have someone hold up a mirror and tell her what they see.

The first activity to clarify your talent is to gather some feedback from those who know you well. The people around you are often best positioned to reflect back to you your own greatness. How could you gather this feedback? The simplest way is to ask them. Call or text close family, friends, and confidants and ask them when they have seen you at your best. I give my clients a more formal activity that goes like this:

First, identify ten to twenty people across your network who have seen you at your best. These could be a combination of past teachers, colleagues, mentors, or friends. You should include family, current significant other, and peers. The greater the sample size, the better. In fact, it is to your benefit to have a cross-section from various phases of your life. As each of these individuals shares their insights, you'll be more likely to see patterns emerge that transcend the past decade or more.

Make a list of each individual's first name, last name, and email address in a spreadsheet.

Next, draft the email request. Your goal is to have each of these individuals send back to you via email three things:

- Three times when they saw you at your best.
- What you were doing that exemplified "your best."
- Why they thought that was you at your best.

If you collect three anecdotes from no less than ten people, you'll have thirty data points to draw from to begin to narrow down your talents.

I'd suggest an email like this:

SAMPLE REQUEST

Dear _____,

In an effort to clarify my talents, I'm working through an assignment and would appreciate your assistance. This involves my contacting ten to twenty people who know me well enough to share specific experiences from my past. I am inviting you to become part of this assignment.

Here is what I need: Please reflect on our past experiences and describe up to three situations where you saw me perform at my very best. It doesn't matter how large or small these events were; so long as you see them as meaningful expressions of my strengths. Please describe these experiences in enough detail that I can understand the circumstances, what I did, and any relevant outcomes. An example is provided below, but use this only as a guide.

Please email these responses back to me no later than ________. Thank you very much for helping with this assignment!

EXAMPLE

One of your strengths is: Your ability to motivate people to work well together.

For example, I think of the time . . .

When we were falling behind schedule on the class project, the stress was building within the group, and the quality of our work was beginning to suffer. You noticed that we were not doing our best work and challenged the group to rethink our approach. You reminded us of what we were capable of doing if we worked more together, and this caused all of us to pause. No one else would have thought to intervene like you did and it made a real difference. In the end, we were all very proud of what we accomplished together and you played a big part in us getting there.

Sincerely,
{Your Name}

Compile all of the individual stories into one document and analyze them for insights into your natural talents. Create a table where you can begin to compile categories of your specific talents along with supporting examples. Try to develop a deeper understanding of specific examples of talents and how they play into what you do best.

NOTE: You will want to follow up with each of your people the day before this is due with a reminder. This should take them no more than five to seven minutes to complete. By the way, if you email your parents, moms loves this stuff. Past clients always get the best feedback from their mothers. Go figure.

Uncomfortable? Sure. It can be slightly awkward to ask people to tell you when they thought you were awesome. But not more uncomfortable than not knowing.

In fact, more often than not clients report that the activity was not only tremendously insightful but also validating, and even helped them build trust and reconnect with past life influences.

In his talk, "Well Done, Thou Good and Faithful Servant," Elder Ronald A. Rasband said, "Sister Rasband, throughout our life together, and Brother Huntsman in my many years of working with him, helped me in this effort. They saw in me gifts and talents that I did not recognize in myself. Choose wisely your friends and mentors, as they will help you identify the gifts and talents you have been blessed with. Listen to your parents and grandparents. They know you well, and we are never too old to take the counsel of those who have already travelled the road we are now on."[2]

How do you find the right mentors? Pay attention to the people God has placed in your circle of friends, associates, and contacts who seem to be invested in your development. Each of us can likely think of a trusted ally, friend, or confidant who will speak the truth, share their perspective, or act as a sounding board. These individuals are invaluable in helping us see beyond ourselves and recognize the value we bring to the world.

I sometimes get the question, "What if people point out things that are draining to me?" No problem. Remember, they are simply pointing out what they thought was you at your best. To them, your best may have been that amazing budget you created or that time you helped them repair their fence. For you, these might have been torturous. That's okay. Your goal should be to review the anecdotes for statements that feel validating, energizing, and authentic. Pay attention to how you feel and listen for the affirming guidance of the Holy Spirit. Which statements make you feel powerful? Which ones light you up? Focus on the things you do that resonate, and especially the ones that seem to consistently pop up at various moments throughout your life. This repetition is often a sign of talent.

The activity brought Sarah, one of my clients, to tears. Prior to seeking this feedback, our coaching sessions had stagnated. She was mired in the quandary of "how do I know this is *really* a talent?" In other words, she wondered if she was the best judge of what she does best.

I challenged her to seek feedback, and the results were overwhelming. The stories and anecdotes from friends, family, colleagues, and others affirmed what she had identified as her talents and added color to her abilities. She had clear moments reflected back to her from when she was at her very best, and walked away with these straightforward talent statements:

- I'm good at connecting with different types of people 1:1 or in small groups.
    - Bringing a smile to someone's face.
    - Having a positive impact on them.
    - Making them feel important.

- I'm a strong problem solver.
    - Partnering with people to find solutions to their challenges.
    - Asking questions and dialoging to analyze and challenge ideas and arrive at the best solution.
    - Being detail-oriented.

- I excel at listening and facilitating.
    - Active and engaged listening to make people feel heard.
    - Synthesizing ideas and translating information to help people understand.
    - Asking questions and challenging individuals to gain clarity and help them build confidence.

I asked her what the feedback exercise was like for her. She said it was vulnerable yet affirming. Most important, she got crystal clear about how she uniquely adds value to those around her.

Remember, it's tough to see the picture when you're in the frame. Others are often well positioned to help you see what you can't. Elder Ronald A. Rasband said, "Consult family members, trusted friends, teachers, and leaders; others often can see in us what we find difficult to see in ourselves."[3]

To this end, one of the greatest gifts you can give another is to tell them what they do very best. Help others see their uniqueness for what it is. Every day we bump into people in our journey through life who are doing what they do best, often without even realizing it. Think of someone right now who is near and dear to you—a friend, family member, fellow Church member, or colleague. What do they do best? When are they "on"? When have you seen them excel? Now go and tell them! Don't wait for a feedback request to share with those closest to you the talents you regularly see in them. Remember: someone has to hold the mirror up to the Mona Lisa for her to see beyond her frame. Let that person be you.

ACTIVITY 2: ENERGY TRACKING

The second way to identify your talents is through active reflection and energy tracking. Clues about your talents lie in the past, in the things you do every day.

First, it's important to recognize that in each moment of each day, you are doing one of two things: you are either making a deposit in your energy account or you are making a withdrawal. There is no in between. We are either doing things that yield energy, joy, and happiness, or we are cashing in on that reservoir of energy to do things that have to get done but that yield almost no joy.

Most of us make more withdrawals than deposits, which in the world of finance is referred to as a deficit. We overdraw our energy accounts! Because we are running energy deficits, we walk around looking drained, feel wiped out when we get home, and don't look forward to the next day. We're in a modern energy crisis.

For example, think about today. Even reading this book, you are either depositing energy or withdrawing it. For those of us who have short attention spans and are highly extroverted, spending time reading this book may require a sacrifice of energy for the ultimate payoff of greater self-knowledge. Others who enjoy the quiet withdraw of reading and reflecting may be making massive investments in their energy account that they plan to draw on to make dinner, run errands, get through the workday, or parent their kids. Shift your mind set to begin thinking of each activity as a **deposit** or a **withdrawal.**

The next step is to pay attention to those moments when you get lost in activity and analyze them. Ask yourself **what** you're doing and **why** you think it's so invigorating—or draining.

A great exercise for identifying talents is to keep a list of your energy deposits and withdrawals by making a T-chart on a piece of paper with a line down the middle, then label the first column "Energy Withdrawals" and the second column "Energy Deposits."

Now open your calendar, or reflect on the previous week, and identify the things that you did that made you feel energized. **Note:** These are not the things that you observed others do that made you feel energized. Rather, they are things you actually did. For example, when I work this activity with teachers, asking them about what things during the past year gave them the most energy, they'll often remark, "Watching my students walk across the stage at graduation." Although this is undoubtedly powerful and rewarding, this says little about their talents. If anything, it highlights the students' resilience and diligence! I'm more interested in things *you* do that yield energy.

Also, focus on getting specific. For example, instead of saying, "checked in with a friend or teammate" or "attended a meeting" clarify *what* about those events you enjoyed. You might say things like "listened to various opinions and summarized them" or "created the agenda and provided structure in the meeting."

Finally, if you don't have a calendar where you track your activities, or if reflecting backward doesn't yield much data, I'll sometimes have my clients track their energy real-time. For the next seven days, end each day by looking at your chart and writing down the things you did that day that energized you and those that drained you. In fact, real-time tracking may be the most accurate method for truly analyzing what you enjoy doing on a regular basis!

Once you have your data points, go item by item, starting with the "energy" side, and unpack each by asking the following:

- What specific activity was I doing that yielded energy?
- What about this activity did I enjoy most?
- Why was it so powerful?

Your goal is to identify a specific formula of action that you do that releases energy and motivation ten times out of ten. For example, a few activities that yielded energy for me this past week included:

- Creating a one-page document for a client that outlined what a quarterly check-in could look like.
- Writing this book!
- Coaching a client on a significant organizational challenge.
- Talking with someone who was launching a business and needed some advice.

If I look at any one of these activities and ask the three questions above—digging deep on the why—the following talent statements emerge:

I'm at my best when I am . . .

- Creating a one-page document for a client that outlines what a quarterly check-in could look like.
    - . . . helping individuals synthesize information that is important to their development.
    - . . . creating tools and resources that help people thrive.
- Writing this book!
    - . . . teaching something I care about for an audience that wants to listen and that benefits their lives.
    - . . . researching information about a topic that is interesting to me and that I can use to benefit others.
- Coaching a client on a significant organizational challenge OR talking with someone who was launching a business and needed some advice.
    - . . . adding value in a way others may not be able to either due to lack of skill, knowledge, or experience.

The sub-bullets above represent raw talents that I focus on using over and over again in a variety of environments to boost energy, increase my chance of success, and feel joy in the work that I do.

Note that this reflection is most easily done with a partner who can listen to the moments when you are at your best and help pick out what makes you feel strong. Doing this in isolation can be difficult, since we often can't see beyond our frame.

For example, a number of years ago I got an email from my friend Katy about her buddy Chris saying he needed some help clarifying his talents and his career path. Then I read more.

Chris was a dentist and hated it. He wanted to do something else, like maybe be a park ranger. I felt a little doubt creep in because three years ago, I got an email from a dentist in Utah who was saddled with mountains of debt but who wanted to reset his career to be an architect. He had a bunch of kids and only one income and the future looked bleak. I was afraid this might be another one of those.

I met Chris at the same breakfast spot where I meet most clients and bought my umpteenth bottle of over-priced water to be a good patron.

Chris was thirty-two, had been a dentist for seven years, and had a wife and a son. Like most dissatisfied dentists, he got into the work because it "runs in the family." Unlike most dentists, he didn't have any debt and his wife also worked as a teacher to bring in income.

I asked Chris how much of his work on a weekly basis he likes and how much he hates. He looked at me weird, so I rephrased the question.

"How much gives you energy and how much drains it?"

He paused again.

"All right," I said, "what is the one thing about it that you enjoy?"

Nothing.

I asked him to give me percentages. "What percentage of the average work week are you doing things that give you energy versus drain it?"

"Zero percent enjoy, 100 percent don't enjoy."

Now to some, that may sound bleak. To me, it sounded like a man ready to reflect. No debt, at the bottom of the valley . . . nowhere to go but up!

"What do you want to do?" I asked.

"I don't know," he said and thought about it for a moment. "Maybe be a park ranger?"

"Why?"

"I love the outdoors, the calm lifestyle, working with people, camping . . . If I were retired today, my wife and I would get in our RV and drive to various national parks. We'd secure seasonal work at the cash register or park entrance and spend our days outdoors and exploring."

Now before you jump to "he should be a park ranger!" there is a key here to figuring out your life's work. No one was put on this earth to be a park ranger, just like no one was really meant to be a basketball player or an engineer. Jobs and careers aren't talents. Talents allow us to be exceptional at jobs and careers, but these aren't one in the same. Talents are the unique way that we do our careers that makes us exceptional basketball players, engineers, or career coaches. Talents are the raw material that can be applied across callings, volunteer roles, family responsibilities and careers, but talents aren't jobs.

The key with Chris' statement—and the same is true for you—is to ask the all-powerful "why." Why do you want to be a park ranger? What about it do you perceive to align with who you are? Then begin to screen the answer for talents. Is it that you love the outdoors? Or is it that it represents freedom and flexibility, which you may be able to find in a different career? Does it activate some of your talents, as you perceive it?

We dug into this reflection and the following talents emerged:

- Taking facts and applying them to real life situations.
- Processing thoughts and ideas internally.
- Be observant and intuitive to the needs of others and put them first to ease their pain and/or increase their comfort.
- Take something I don't know how to do, learn more about it, and do it.
- Do something to contribute or add value to people.
- Focus on a task 100 percent until it's done.

- Think through the processes unemotionally to find a solution or make a decision.
- Utilize positivity to motivate or inspire others to action.

A few things occurred to me. First, dentistry wasn't a terrible fit considering he loved working with his hands, solving problems, connecting with humans, doing something to contribute to people's lives, focus, and so on.

In fact, it seemed like a great fit. What was missing?

"I hate the quotas. The impersonal nature of it. I feel disconnected from people and get a ton of stress from showing up and working with people in pain who are generally afraid of the dentist," he said.

Makes sense, so I sent Chris away with a goal:

Run an informational interview with three people: 1) a professor of dentistry (given his penchant for motivating and inspiring people), 2) radiation therapy (his mom passed away from cancer and this profession seemed to align with his passion to solve this problem), and 3) RV sales and/or outdoor work.

The goal? Ask the following questions:

1. What do you do for a living?
2. What does that look like on a daily basis?
3. Why do you do it?
4. How did you get there?
5. BONUS: What recommendations would you have for me if I wanted to pursue that route?

We set up a session for four weeks later.

Now this is where most people flounder. There's something about connecting with others that stops people, whether it's the discomfort of reaching out to people or breaking out of their routine.

Not Chris.

He came back four weeks later but something had changed. In fact, he was a totally different guy. Energy was high, he seemed lighter, and he was confident. He reported back:

"So I met a guy in radiation therapy. The worked seemed really interesting and I left feeling pretty optimistic about it.

And then I met with a former professor in dentistry and that changed everything."

"What?! What changed?" I asked.

"As this professor described his work every day—teaching, supporting, coaching on the job, mentoring students, assisting with procedures in clinic, solving problems . . . I lit up. I felt it. Totally energizing."

I was pumped for him, but more important he was pumped for himself.

I said, "Wow. You seem like a different guy."

He told me his wife and family had said the same thing. But here's the real kicker:

His day-to-day job running procedures and filling quotas was more meaningful. Why? Because he was approaching it with *purpose.* Suddenly, every appointment was an opportunity to learn something new that he may soon be teaching and to put a different experience/anecdote in his tool belt.

In the meantime, the professor he interviewed ended up introducing him around right then and there to colleagues, including ones who sat on the recruiting committee.

Boom.

Chris identified clear talents through a reflection process and began to look for opportunities to magnify them more regularly.

Remember, the things you do well may be thinking talents (the way you conceptualize or think through an idea), feeling talents (the way you relate to or connect with people), or doing talents (the way you organize your world or accomplish work). All three are valid.

Talents are like your fingerprints. They're unique to you. The combination of talents you possess differentiates you from the other 7.3 billion people in the world.

Capturing and charting is a key to identifying them.

Can *anyone* identify talent?

Are youth capable of identifying talents?

Definitely.

A few years back my daughter "volun-told" me to present at her sixth-grade career day in middle school. I'm not convinced she actually knew what I did for a living, nor that any of her peers would grasp the concept of a leadership consultant and career coach, so I decided instead to teach them something of value.

I started off by asking them to raise their hands if they had any talents. Every hand went up. One identified skating, another drawing. A feisty young Texan in the corner self-identified as a talented bow-hunter. We talked about the power of talents and how to identify them, and I gave them a list of talents like the list below and asked them to quietly reflect on two or three talents they felt they possessed based on past success, feedback from others, and their "gut instinct."

The results were awesome. These sixth graders were able to confidently identify and articulate their talents and give examples of those talents in action. "But were they *really* talents, Dustin, or simply things they aspired to but hadn't yet developed?" Who cares! And who am I to judge?

Likewise, I recently spoke to an auditorium of seven hundred parents and teenagers, all high school juniors and seniors. At one point in the session I posed the question, "Can teenagers figure out their talents and values? Or are they just too young?" The reaction was interesting. I'd break the audience down into three groups. The first group were those parents who furrowed their brow, shook their head "no," and muttered to me or the people around them things like, "No way. They're too young. They don't have enough life experience." The second group were parents who nodded emphatically, likely because their teenagers know their talents or because they simply have faith in the next generation. The last group were all of the teenagers, all of whom nodded "yes!" and some who exclaimed out loud, "Yes! We can do this!" They said it almost as a plea, like, "Give us a chance and let us surprise you. We just need some help." The real irony was to see groups one and three sitting side-by-side—parents shaking their head "no" while their son or daughter sitting next to them nodded their head "yes!" Having helped people from ten years old to sixty-five figure out their talents, I'm here to tell you the answer is "yes." Anyone can figure this out with the right help and guidance. Give them a chance!

In fact, I'd suggest that our youth—and children—may be more aware of their talents than many adults, particularly because they often aren't yet hindered by the self-doubt and fear that plagues many of us in our pursuit of utilizing our talents. A theory I have on talent is that we most purely pursue our talents before we ever go to school. Think about it—kids are shameless in pursuing what brings them joy. They want to dance, sing, play, perform, build, create, and question. They are often uninhibited and totally authentic. A friend of mind remarked to me, "This is so true. It is such a pleasure to watch my four-year-old creating art and playing music. He's not evaluating it for whether it is good or bad. He's just experiencing the joy of doing his thing." It's not until many children enter school and are told how to behave, at what time, and where that those inhibitions grow and the talent discovery process may slow. All the more reason that our children and youth need an advocate to help them along on their talent journey.

ADDITIONAL HELP FOR IDENTIFYING TALENTS

Aside from the feedback of "close others" and directed self-reflection, the Lord has given us many tools to help us identify our inherent abilities. Remember—He wants us to use these talents to benefit humankind.

PRAYER

One of the most fundamental ways to discover talent is through earnest prayer and pondering. Prayer coupled with reflection is a powerful formula for getting clear about your unique identity.

One young man named Spencer said this:

> I've always wondered if I had any real talent. I was weak in most things such as sports, dance, looks, and being a gentle person. I had different capabilities though. I could sing, play a few instruments, memorize, write stories, do well in school, and draw. I thought I never had a specific field I thought I was REALLY good in. I prayed to know what I was really good at and how I could develop it. In the end the Spirit helped me realize

that my talent was not limited to a certain field. Perhaps my talent was being able to learn to do different things! I felt better about myself then. I'm sharing this because I know a lot of youth experience the same thing. An advice I would add to this list would be to list down all the things you can do, even if you're not extremely good at it. You'll be surprised at how much you can do! Then, think of ways you can use them to serve others. It's more fulfilling than looking down on yourself. See yourself through God's eyes. See your potential.

Prayer is fundamental to knowing how God sees you. Remember Enoch in the book of Moses? At the young-ish age of sixty-five, Enoch received a call from God to preach repentance to the people. Enoch, feeling inadequate, bowed himself before the Lord in prayer and suggested several reasons he couldn't magnify that call:

1. He was a lad.
2. The people hated him.
3. He was slow of speech.

The Lord then gave Enoch a glimpse of his potential, in Moses 6:32–34 (emphasis added):

> And the Lord said unto Enoch: Go forth and do as I have commanded thee, and no man shall pierce thee. **Open thy mouth, and it shall be filled, and I will give thee utterance, for all flesh is in my hands, and I will do as seemeth me good.**
>
> Say unto this people: Choose ye this day, to serve the Lord God who made you.
>
> Behold my Spirit is upon you, wherefore all thy words will I justify; **and the mountains shall flee before you, and the rivers shall turn from their course; and thou shalt abide in me, and I in you; therefore walk with me.**

Wow. A self-proclaimed "lad" who is slow of speech and has very little buy-in from the people around him would one day move mountains. And he did!

A young woman named Christina shared this anecdote about the power of prayer in identifying her talents:

> I have always been terrible at sports so I kind of ruled them out as a gift. I stuck with piano and violin and decided that was the only thing I was good at. This year my mom convinced me to try out for swim team. I made it into the advanced group and many of the parents as well as my coach were really surprised I had never swam competitively. After I told my coach this she said "Really? Wow you are just really natural in the water." Heavenly Father gives us many more gifts than we can imagine. If i had ruled out all sports because I was not able to do some, I would not have discovered this hidden talent and had such a great experience. Pray to know your gifts and in His time, in His way, he will tell you.

Through earnest prayer, the Lord will help you identify your talents. Ask Him to help you be in tune enough with the Spirit to recognize those innate abilities. Reflect with Him at the end of the day on the things you did especially well and ask Him how He would like you to use those gifts to the benefit of others. If these talents came with us from the premortal world, and if He is the Father of us all—the One who gave them to us—then one of His greatest concerns must be our discovery, development, and active application of these gifts. Ask God!

PATRIARCHAL BLESSINGS

Last year I was invited to a ward in Las Vegas to share more about the concept of talents during a fifth Sunday class. In preparation, I created a list of other ways to identify talents, including patriarchal blessings. In the spirit of not suggesting something I myself haven't used, I wondered if there was anything in my own blessing that would tell me more about the talents I possess.

I sat down one morning to review my blessing, which I received when I was seventeen, and was shocked to see a talent written so plainly that I had never noticed before. It stated, "You have the attributes to present yourself in a manner that people will listen" and "you have a testimony to convince people of the truth of your message."

There, right before me, were clear clues about the talents God may have blessed me with and their potential use for good, pending my obedience and righteousness. In fact, I wish I had given that statement more attention when I was pursuing seminary teaching as a career twenty years ago!

Certainly, patriarchal blessings hold insights into who we were before we came to earth, who we are now, and our divine potential.

From the Church's website, we learn that patriarchal blessings are more than a declaration of lineage. They "contain personal revelation and instructions from Heavenly Father, who knows our strengths, weaknesses, and eternal potential. Patriarchal blessings may contain promises, admonitions, and warnings. Those who follow the counsel in their patriarchal blessing will be less likely to go astray or be misled."[4] These blessings provide insight into who we are at our best.

Review your patriarchal blessing with these questions in mind:

- What does God tell me about my unique identity?
- What action verbs stand out as things He'd like me to do? What talents will I need to make those things happen?
- What promises do I see as a result of exercising my talents?

You may choose to make a fresh copy of your blessing and use a highlighter and pen to annotate your answers to the questions above. Like me, you will be astounded by the insights God has given us in these blessings.

THE SCRIPTURES, MODERN-DAY LEADERS, AND ANCESTORS

One gap in identifying talents seems to be an inability to articulate what it is we do best. Given that's it easier to identify the talents of others, one suggestion may be to look for talents you share in common with prophets in the scriptures, modern-day leaders, and even ancestors.

Eldred G. Smith, former Patriarch to the Church, gave this counsel: "Everyone has inherent talents. From a study of your genealogy [family history], find the talents you have inherited by the things you like to do, and do easily, that some of your ancestors have done. Then become an expert or a specialist in some phase of that field. The Lord will bless your efforts in your studies and in your daily work."[5]

I'm not particularly adept at forging iron, building wagon wheels, or pulling handcarts like many of my pioneer ancestors, but my great-great-grandfather was a principal and educator in southern Utah when the Saints settled there, and I have to believe that my drive to educate, train, and help people, particularly in the education sector, is part of my DNA as a descendant of Mads Peter Sorenson.

In analyzing your ancestry, or reading about former- or latter-day prophets, what talents do you recognize that may give you insights about your own gifts? You may not have to look far. In fact, you may share talents with your parents, grandparents, siblings, cousins or other close kin.

Likewise, as you study the scriptures and the lives of modern-day leaders, you may see in them some of your talents, clearly articulated. Adam was obedient and hard-working while Eve was loyal, insightful, and bold. Joseph of Egypt was diligent, visionary, and had a talent for interpretation and Moses was a leader. Ruth was confident and kind. Mary, the mother of Jesus, had a believing heart. And the Savior embodied all great talents, abilities, and characteristics. Indeed, a thorough study of the life of Jesus Christ might give you more clues of your own natural abilities that anything else.

Search the scriptures diligently for clues about your talents. Prayer may be the way that we solicit heavenly help on this quest to discover who we really are, but the answer might lie in the word of God.

DISCOVER YOUR TALENTS

Remember, talents come in many varieties. The result of utilizing talents is joy, ease, happiness, energy, and satisfaction. So ask yourself, "What makes me happy? When do I feel most at ease? What comes easy to me? When do I feel natural?"

Discovering talents is the journey of a lifetime. What I've presented here are only a few ways to pin down what you do very best, but remember that the greatest insight will come from the Holy Ghost, usually in the quiet moments of the day. I'll often pose this question to my clients: "What recurring patterns of thought do you have about what you do best, especially during quiet and often unintuitive moments of the day, like when you are in the shower, mowing the lawn, or commuting to work?" Pay attention to those "recurring patterns." Your talents have been with you since you were born and will manifest consistently over time. Each time you use them, the Holy Ghost will affirm that effort and you'll feel a desire to use them again.

Alas, discovering your talents is only the first step to becoming who God intended for you to be. Talents take time to develop. In fact, the energy we put toward talents—instead of fixing what's "broken" or left out—will yield huge results. In the next chapter, we'll discuss how to develop your talents into sources of power that you can rely on to achieve a desired outcome for the benefit of humankind. Buckle up!

NOTES

1. J. K. Rowling Quotes. (n.d.). BrainyQuote.com; accessed March 26, 2021, frombrainyquote.com/quotes/j_k_rowling_454004.
2. Ronald A. Rasband, "Well Done Thou Good and Faithful Servant," Churchofjesuschrist.org, March 23, 2020.
3. Ronald A. Rasband, "You've Got Talent." *New Era*, July 2018, churchofjesuschrist.org/study/new-era/2018/07/youve-got-talent?lang=eng.
4. "Patriarchal Blessings," Gospel Topics, churchofjesuschrist.org/study/manual/gospel-topics/patriarchal-blessings?lang=eng.
5. Eldred G. Smith, "Decision," *Ensign*, May 1978, 29.

CHAPTER 5

Developing Your Talents

"Hide not your talents, they for use were made,
What's a sundial in the shade?"[1]

—BENJAMIN FRANKLIN

I can vividly remember the moment when I first discovered and articulated my talents.

I was sitting in a professional development workshop as an employee at the University of Nevada–Las Vegas (UNLV). The instructor had just described talent in a way I'd never considered—as a raw, innate ability; something we do at a high level and consistently well.

He asked us to reflect on moments when we were at our best, and my mind immediately jumped to teaching. In my role at the time I was directing leadership development efforts with students and teaching courses in the leadership minor on campus. My mind flashed to the one-on-one conversations I'd had as an advisor and to teaching classes and workshops on a weekly basis. As a result, I generated the following statements:

I feel strong when I . . .

- Help individuals synthesize information that is important to their development.

- Prepare a lesson with good questions about something relevant to me and for people who want to listen.
- Facilitate and teach something I care about for an audience that wants to listen and that benefits their life.
- Research information about a topic that is interesting to me and that I can use to benefit others.
- Can use my competitive edge and talents to take something that is good and make it better than it was before I got to it.
- Observe a method for solving a problem or dilemma and then replicate the method, improving it or enhancing it to make it better.

The facilitator reminded us that talents make us feel **strong.** He asked if that was true of each of these statements, which it was. We then did some brief wrap-up and the session ended, leaving me with a big question that you may have as well.

Now what?

Identifying talent is only step one. The real power of talents comes in developing them into something greater—multiplying them for the Lord. Remember in the parable of the talents in Matthew 25 that the great differentiator between those who were welcomed into the "joy of the Lord" and the servant who was cast out was the effort each made to develop the talents the Master had given them: "Then he that had received the five talents *went and traded with the same, and made them other five talents.* And likewise he that had received two, *he also gained other two.* But he that had received one *went and digged in the earth, and hid his lord's money*" (verses 16–18; emphasis added).

Over the past decade of coaching people on their talents, I've created a number of exercises to help them develop their talents. Several of these are detailed below. However, the most important principle in developing your talents is also the simplest: use them. Intentionally and often. I say "intentionally" because we actually use our talents daily, albeit without realizing it. Remember that the great paradox of talent is that these things come so naturally to us that we may not even realize we're using them. Those who turn their talents into true strengths are focused and *intentional* about applying them to every situation.

Talents are the raw material that makes us great in various activities. Using my talents above as an example, "synthesizing information to help people" could be used in counseling a church member, coaching my children, listening to a friend, consulting an organization, or simply cutting through a load of content to identify the key points. Talents are transferable, and opportunities are all around us to develop and deploy what we do best.

Allow me to provide another example. This one comes from a post I wrote on the subject of using our talents as the foundation of a successful career. In the post I argued the point that the Lord *does* care what we do for a living because He likely prefers that we use our talents for the betterment of mankind. A commenter said the following:

> I wonder if the quote should be "The Lord doesn't care what you do for a living as long as you do it well AND can support your family." I saw a job once that aligned with my passion (motorcycles) so closely it was freakish. The only problem? It paid about $10.00 an hour.
>
> So in theory I agree with your post. The Lord wants you to use your talents and wants you to be happy. Why should your job be excluded? But if your talents and passions won't be borne by the market then you could be out of luck.

In response, I said:

> I think we often confuse the catalyst of our happiness as the subject of our work rather than the way we arrive at it. Talents are the way we arrive at the outcomes!
>
> Let me clarify with an example. I recently built a board and batten for our kitchen wall. I loved building it. I was even passionate about it, losing myself in the project, feeling fluid and natural as I did it, and coming away with more energy after completing it than before I started. One could argue that I should go into carpentry because that sounds like a talent. However, the board and batten happened to be the "subject" of my talent but was not necessarily my talent. My true talent may have been using my innate ability to take something that was average and

visualizing a better product, then breaking it down into tangible steps to get there. It turns out that I use this same skill each time I coach someone in their leadership or career and I get the same energy as I did building a board and batten.

My point is that motorcycles may have been the subject toward which the commenter was using his talents but not necessarily the talent itself. Sure, he may love the actual pieces of metal that make up a motorcycle, but there are likely other talents or skills that he was using when working on them that released some passion/energy that he could replicate in other lines of work.

I only use this as an example to say that I believe the Lord has given us talents that are more formulaic and skill-focused than subject-oriented, and that it is life's quest to identify those talents and use them over and over in as many arenas as possible, the result of which would also be increased energy, satisfaction, and productivity in our own lives.

Developing your talents is a journey, not an event!

Below are a few methods for more intentional talent development.

ACTIVITY #1: CURRENT ACTIVITY AUDIT

Opportunities for using our talents lie all around us. Whether we use them to organize or clean the house, plan an activity or meal, teach a class, contribute to an event, coach a friend or family member, or simply understand and empathize with another person, God puts us in a position every day (if we let Him) to utilize our abilities. Thus, the first activity I use to help individuals develop their talents is to audit the opportunities around them.

Using the table on the following page, list the three activities you did this past week (or in an average week) that gave you the most energy. In the next column, list the three activities you do the most, whether or not they utilize talents. There may be some overlap. Finally identify the percentage of the time (say, weekly) that you currently use your talents.

TABLE 1

Top Three Energizing Activities	Top Three Activities I Spend the Most Time/Energy Doing	Percentage of the Week That I'm Using My Talents

Now analyze opportunities around you to use your talents more often. In what activities *could you have used your talents?* Set a goal and get specific.

TABLE 2

In what new situations can you put yourself in to use your talents more? Who do you need to talk to?
How can you change your weekly schedule or the order you do things in to maximize your talent?

Developing your talents might be as simple as beginning to use them more regularly. Don't ever miss an opportunity to do what you do best!

ACTIVITY #2: TALENT DEVELOPMENT PLAN

Remember: talents are the raw material we use to contribute to the world. But they are just that—raw. In this activity, take a moment to reflect on the knowledge and skill you might add to those talents to maximize them. *Knowledge* is often grouped into two categories: factual and experiential. *Factual knowledge* includes content you learn from books, articles, talks, classes or other mediums. *Experiential knowledge* consists of things you learn by doing them such as riding a bike, grilling a hamburger, or learning to swim. Although there is some overlap between the two and you could certainly learn to grill a burger by reading a tome on 1,001 Techniques for Grilling, most knowledge of this kind is gained by doing.

Skills are aptitudes—much like talents—but they are not inherent. This makes them transferable or teachable. Skills are things you can show someone else how to do. So, you could teach someone how to write a lesson plan, play the piano, or dance. Can these things also be talents? Sure, someone could be a gifted pianist or dancer. But if the output or action is learned, not innate, it's likely a skill.

With this in mind, we develop our talents by intentionally investing time in increasing our knowledge and skill with regard to that talent. For example, if someone is talented at "creating and executing a plan of action," they might do the following to grow that talent:

Talent: Creating and executing a plan of action.

Knowledge: Watch a YouTube video on executing an action plan (a quick search revealed three right off the top), read a book on goal setting, or attend a workshop that teaches strategic planning.

Skill: Learn how to use Excel or another software (project management) to build action plans.

The goal is to take raw ability and layer on knowledge and skill to make it stronger. If you're talented in connecting with people, read a book on empathy. If you're a natural analyzer, learn and practice a problem-solving methodology. If you retain information naturally well, download a memory app to strengthen that talent!

You can also develop your talent by applying the same talent toward different areas of life. In other words, in deploying your talent toward areas of interest you can grow that talent in new and dynamic ways. The key here would be to add knowledge and skill in new arenas that leverage the talent. Let's take an example. Using the same example from before ("creating and executing a plan of action"), they might add knowledge and skills to that talent as follows:

- **Talent:** Creating and executing a plan of action.
- **Knowledge:** Reading a book on how to bake a cake, watching or attending a course on baking techniques, or studying how various ingredients might interplay with each other.
- **Skill:** Learning how to grease a pan, mix ingredients, or operate an oven.

The result would be that this individual developed their talent by aiming it toward baking, with a focus on increasing knowledge and skill in that area. Note that this same individual might redirect that talent toward building a business, teaching a dance class, or investing. The knowledge and skills are fluid, but the talent at the root remains the same.

Opportunities to develop your talents are endless. When I discovered an innate ability to facilitate dialogue in the moment to help a group work through a problem, I attached myself to a mentor who was much better than I was at that talent and learned all I could. We would co-facilitate sessions together and unpack the experience after the fact. He gave me feedback, built my confidence, and shared techniques for being a stronger facilitator. To this day, he remains one of the individuals who taught me the most about how to read a room, move a group forward, and direct people toward clear outcomes, even when the process feels murky.

Instructions: Identify the talents you have and then the activities you are interested in doing to turn them into strengths. These could be reading a book, Googling a topic, attending a seminar, shadowing an expert, or seeking coaching in a certain area.

TABLE 3

Talent	What I Need to Do to Develop It into a Strength (Knowledge and Strength)

MY ACTION STEP THIS WEEK

Now choose one thing you will do this week. Note that this isn't one thing per talent, but simply *one thing*. The best way to identify talents is with focused effort delivered consistently over time!

TABLE 4

My Action Step:

ACTIVITY #3: TALENT CONNECTION

Your talents are on display all the time. Because talents are innate, we often don't notice when we're using them. This doesn't mean they aren't there, but rather that we don't have the awareness to recognize them.

Taking some time to reflect on moments during the week when your talents came alive can be a powerful activity for increasing your self-awareness. You will also be in a better position to intentionally deploy those talents in the same situations in the future.

Instructions: Write your talents in the column on the left. Use the talents you discovered in chapter 4. Then reflect on what those talents allow you to do. What's the impact? Last, identify when you most recently put them to work.

TABLE 5

Talent	What This Talent Allows Me to Do	When/Where I Recently Used This Talent
Example: active listening.	Understand another's perspective to individualize a solution for them.	Mediating a conflict between two friends on Friday by asking great questions and listening for the core issues!

Talent	What This Talent Allows Me to Do	When/Where I Recently Used This Talent

ACTIVITY #4: TALENT AND DIFFICULTY

Talents release energy. After using talents, people often describe their emotions as powerful, fluid, natural, strong, or in control. On the other hand, weaknesses or tasks that aren't innate often feel clumsy, unnatural, difficult, slow, or painful. I feel this way anytime I have to manage my accounting books, navigate a ton of quantitative data, or run to the grocery store to find something obscure at my wife's request, like lime juice or spices. And yet, we all have to do things we don't enjoy.

Talents give us a new way to approach things we otherwise wouldn't enjoy doing. In a previous job, I coordinated a leadership internship program. Every spring, I had to read through more than 140 internship applications in a two-week period. I hated it. Reading these applications would constantly find its way from to-do list to to-do list, day after day. I'd punt it from my morning schedule to the afternoon, only to find reasons that afternoon to avoid its misery and punt it to the next day.

Because I have a talent for doing things better than they were done before, and in an effort to do anything I could to make this more bearable, I made a game of the tedium. I would set a forty-five-minute timer to read through as many of these applications as I could. I would then take a fifteen-minute break to walk the office, connecting with colleagues and boosting my energy before returning to my dungeon and resetting the timer to accomplish more than I did the previous hour. The subtle sense of self-competition activated my "competition" talent and desire to "do things better than I did before." The breaks to connect with people and build relationships ignited my talent for relating with others. I won't say that I grew to *adore* application review, but I certainly walked away with more energy than I would have otherwise, and likely accomplished the task with greater effectiveness.

Talents can be utilized to make difficult tasks less difficult. Get creative and apply them any chance you get.

Instructions: Identify a specific task in your life with which you have difficulty. The difficulty could be a problem at work, a challenge in your relationships, or simply a redundant task you have to do to keep your life moving forward. Now look back at The Talent Connection activity. Paying attention to what you said each of your talents allows you to do, think about how you could use your talents to approach that difficulty in a different, more productive way. Identify four talents and specific ways in which you could use those themes to deal with this situation.

TABLE 6

Difficulty	Talents

EXAMPLE

Using activities like the ones above plus a dose of intentional effort, I took one of my talents from my original list more than a decade ago and built my entire profession on it.

During that initial workshop at UNLV, I reflected on several interactions I had with students during the week when I had helped mirror back to them things I heard them say that might help them make difficult decisions in their lives. From that reflection, I came up with the following talent statement:

> I feel strong when I help individuals synthesize information that is important to their development.

Recognizing that I had a raw ability to cut through the complexity any synthesize the most important information for people, I signed up for a two-day coaching course to help me improve my active listening, questioning, and other coaching skills. In the training, I learned that active listening happens on three different levels:

- Level 1 is listening to both what the other person is saying and to my own internal thoughts about what they are saying. It includes listening to my own thoughts, feelings, and interpretations. Most of us listen at a level 1 most of the time. We interpret what the other person is saying through our own filter, making sense of what they say within our own context.
- Level 2 is focused listening, which is a laser-like focus on what the person is saying. In level 2, we focus only on what the speaker is saying and block out all other distractions. We listen only to the words and don't seek to interpret them.
- Level 3 is a soft, receptive focus that encompasses everything around you, your senses, and your environment. This is the most powerful for coaching because it's listening for what's **not** being said. Level 3 is about listening to the undercurrent, the body language, the energy shifts, and the mood in the room and naming that. It's listening for the sub-context and intent.

Understanding these levels of listening helped me to realize that my greatest value-add and "synthesis of information" will come from levels 2 and 3, listening to exactly what is being said *and* what is not being said explicitly but what lies just underneath the surface of the conversation.

The next thing I did was to acquire a "coaching notebook," a lined notebook I could use to capture what I heard (and didn't hear!) that would be important for peoples' development. I studied articles online about how to capture notes more effectively and came up with a system where a "star" represents something I thought as I listened to the individual talk, a "dash" represents something they said that was important or potentially powerful, and a "small square" represents an action step or next step they might need to do to progress.

Finally, I began to invest in own knowledge and understanding of theories of human behavior, especially regarding career and leadership. I read more than one hundred books in three years, subscribed to articles and podcasts, and devoured literature related to common topics in coaching—conflict, self-awareness, mindsets, goals, leadership, management, teamwork, and more. Increasing my knowledge gave me a bank of models and theories to draw from to provide value to those I coached.

Notice that these activities happened over a series of *years,* not weeks. Intentional talent development takes time. However, an opportunity came to fruition in 2012 when I was hired to direct leadership development efforts for a charter school network in the Houston area and one of my main tasks was to coach more than two hundred people in the organization. I used the coaching skills I had acquired, combined with notetaking techniques and my knowledge of leadership and human behavior, and began to coach people regularly to achieve better results in their jobs and lives. After three years of working for this organization, I left my job and launched Proof Leadership Group, a leadership consultancy focused on coaching and training leaders how to build high-performing organizational cultures. Now a staple of what I do is coaching, which all traces back to identifying that talent many years ago and going "all in" on developing the knowledge and skills I would need to make that the core of what I do.

I followed a similar process with my talents for research, planning, teaching, facilitating, and competition. I learned structures, systems, knowledge, processes, and models to figure out how to grow these raw abilities into something I could use to add value to the world. You can do the same!

Be intentional about analyzing ways to maximize what you do best. Remember in the parable of the talents that the Lord praised those who multiplied their talents and chastised those who didn't. We're given these talents to bless not only our own lives but those of the people around us.

Opportunities to develop our talents are all around us if we will focus our efforts and be intentional.

NOTE

1. Benjamin Franklin, *Poor Richard's Almanack: Being the Almanacks of 1733, 1749, 1756, 1757, 1758*. First written under the name of Richard Saunders (Garden City, N.Y: Doubleday, Doran and Co., 1928).

CHAPTER 6

Magnifying Talents

"Use the talents you possess, for the woods would be quiet if no birds sang except the best."

—UNKNOWN

About a year ago I got an email from a guy—we'll call him Jake—who had been connected to me by his brother-in-law. In the email, he said:

> So my story is a bit crazy. I started school in instrumental performance playing the trumpet. I later switched to psychology for a year before I served a mission for The Church of Jesus Christ of Latter-day Saints. I served in Los Angeles and worked my butt off! There I realized how passionate I am about people. Everything about me turned into this human-loving connection seeker!
>
> Since being home, I've struggled with school a lot. I thought a business degree would be good, got talked into trying computer science, and got discouraged and worked on generals unsuccessfully. I've had a number of very different jobs since I've been home, but I'm now working full time selling cars as of two weeks ago. I'd love to talk with you!

First off, I love getting emails like this. All I see when I read this is an individual teeming with talent that may be undiscovered or undeveloped. We set up a time to talk and hopped on the phone.

After hearing a bit of his story, I led with the same question I always start with: what do you do best?

He struggled a bit, so I asked him to describe moments—on his mission, in school, or on the job—when he's felt energy. Remember, energy is a hallmark of talent.

He described connecting with people on his mission and using that same talent in his current job. He discussed teaching, motivating, inspiring, and helping people apply the gospel to their lives. The more he talked, the clearer it became that he needed to be in a people-oriented, teaching-focused career with an emphasis on self-discovery, development, and spirituality.

I stated the obvious, then asked him why he didn't do it.

Self-doubt and fear . . . the usual suspects.

And yet, the key to more joy and clarity in his path lies in identifying, developing, and maximizing his talents *for the benefit of humankind.*

To what end should we use our talents? Or, said another way, where should we aim them?

FOR THE BENEFIT OF ALL

Sam Brannan, an early leader in the Church, was left to figure out how to move the Saints from New York to California as the Saints began to move across the plains to Utah. He chartered a ship to San Francisco, California, and sought to persuade Brigham Young to settle permanently on the coast of California.

When Brigham declared his intention to move the Saints to the Rocky Mountains, Brannan stayed in San Francisco, directing his considerable talents at two goals: business and making money.

Was he successful? Surely. He became the first millionaire in California and is credited with being the first to publicize the Gold Rush. He invested in large tracts of land and several businesses and became very wealthy. But, as President James E. Faust noted, "when he died he was alone, broken physically, spiritually, and financially. For sixteen months no one claimed his body. Eventually it was placed in San Diego's Mount Hope Cemetery. Sam Brannan accomplished much in his life, but in the end he paid a terrible price for not honoring his priesthood stewardship and having failed to follow the prophet of God."[1]

Brannan made a fundamental mistake, using his considerable talents for his own gain and neglecting the opportunity to also build the kingdom of God. Note the word "also." Talents should certainly be used to provide for our families, attain financial security, and thrive at work. But these are not the end of talents; they are a by-product.

Remember in the parable of the talents that the Master wasn't any more pleased with the servant who only earned two talents than the one who earned five. It seems that God is less concerned with the outcome of our talents and more so with the active development and utilization of them.

And for what purpose does God give talents to humankind?

For the benefit of all.

Sure talents can benefit you, your career, and your quality of life. People sometimes ask me, "But isn't the pursuit and use of talents inherently selfish because they give you more satisfaction?" Yes, they give you more satisfaction, but they benefit the world in a tremendous way at the same time and that is their intended use!

In Doctrine and Covenants 82:18–19, the Lord is clear about the endgame for talents:

> And all this for the benefit of the church of the living God, that every man may improve upon his talent, **that every man may gain other talents, yea, even an hundred fold, to be cast into the Lord's storehouse, to become the common property of the whole church**—
>
> Every man **seeking the interest of his neighbor**, and doing all things with an eye single to the glory of God. (emphasis added)

Elder Henry D. Taylor of the Seventy said, "God has granted to each of us gifts, talents, and abilities, with the hope and expectation that we will increase and use them—not for selfish purposes, but for the benefit of others. Let us never forget that these gifts are given 'that all may be profited thereby.'"[2] I suggest that service in the Church offers unlimited opportunities for the unselfish use of our God-given gifts and talents.

We have a talented project manager in our stake. He's organized, knows how to create effective processes, and is people oriented. Members share stories about his multi-page instruction sheets for elders quorum service projects. He knows how to get stuff done! A few years back when a hurricane hit the Houston area, this man was instrumental in organizing work groups, disseminating tools, and influencing the cleanup in a positive way. If you were on his jobsite it just felt different. People weren't clustering in the same part of the house, the trash on the curb was sorted, and the work got done efficiently. The difference? His talents!

Likewise, I know a man who is articulate, creative, and a doer. For his day job he aims his talents at marketing and is tremendously effective at it. In the Church, he's been assigned everything from a high councilor to a counselor in the bishopric to an elders quorum president and thrives wherever he is. As a high councilor, he was charged with emphasizing temple and family history work and the effort took off. Again, the difference was his application of talent.

As a final example, my wife has many gifts and talents. She's positive, organized, builds friendships easily, and knows how to execute. She's a natural leader and has a magnetic personality. Anywhere she serves she adds value and elevates the role. In the PTA, she's made things happen for our local elementary school that would never have happened otherwise. She's rallied parents, raised money, coordinated events, shown gratitude for teachers, and acquired shades for the playground. When aimed at building God's kingdom, her talents make her an amazing member missionary, fluidly sharing her beliefs with anyone she comes in contact with. She builds relationships in the Young Women organization in our branch, helps organize and execute camp for the young women each year, and is a friend to everyone in our Spanish-speaking unit, in spite of the fact that she doesn't speak much Spanish! Her talents help her thrive in the world, but their impact is magnified when directed at building the kingdom.

In addition, talents can benefit those outside of the Church community, or even just our families. I once got an interesting question on a webinar I participated in on talents. A woman asked something to the effect of, "Do talents also include musical or artistic ability? I feel like I have these talents but I sometimes don't develop them because I feel guilty doing so, knowing that my time and attention should be more focused on doing family history work, serving in my calling, my other family duties, etc. I feel guilty taking time to practice my artistic abilities."

My response was two-pronged:

1. Yes! Musical and artistic abilities are absolutely talents.
2. This question hurts my soul. We, the world, are missing out. We're sitting here thinking, "I wish I had some beautiful art to look at or some calming music to listen to." We need you!

We have to use our talents. Remember in the parable of the talents, the development and growing of these abilities yields the joy of the Lord. Moreover, the world is a beautiful tapestry of talent that suffers when people hold back. Don't hold back!

Utilizing your talents isn't a future proposition. It's here and now! Opportunities to use your talents to benefit others are everywhere, but if they go untapped, they will disappear.

TALENTS ARE THE HOW

Remember, talents are the HOW of the work we do. If you were to gather every Relief Society president, bishop, Sunday School teacher, or Primary worker throughout the entire Church into one massive room, you would undoubtedly find that every one of them is doing their calling in a different way. That's by design.

Each has different talents and abilities, different intuition and aptitude. Thus, each will approach the same work totally differently. The result is a unique and individualized approach to doing God's work.

I was talking to my wife a while back about this concept of using talents to differentiate yourself in your calling, and she said, "Give me a real example of putting your talents to work in a calling."

I said, "Okay, give me a calling. Any calling."

She played along. "All right, you're now a ward clerk. No longer a member of the stake presidency. How would your talents transfer?"

"Well, I'd use the first six months just learning my duty. I'd become a bit robotic initially for the sake of ensuring I'm doing a good job. But very quickly, I'd begin looking for opportunities to synthesize data around ministering or expired temple recommends. I'd then go to a bishopric meeting and ask for some time to present what I found in a meaningful way so they could use their keys to counsel about what to do about it. I'd research, synthesize, and present over and over and over again."

You are not your calling, or your job, or your role as a youth or parent. You are a unique, dynamic individual who happens to serve in those roles. Bring yourself to your work!

I'm thinking of my good friend Randy, the greatest stake executive secretary I've known. He could have simply filled assignments to set appointments for the stake president and track information and action steps, but he went above and beyond to bring his talents to bear. In presidency meetings he would actively speak up and offer counsel and insight. He was selected to speak in stake and ward conferences because of his knowledge, perspective, and commitment to the gospel. He's a gifted orator, and participated in stake musical programs. He's a tremendous example of someone who brought himself to the calling, instead of becoming the calling.

Talents also determine your unique approach to work. For example, I have a good friend who is a dentist. His job description may read like this:

- Clean teeth
- Do root canals
- Run a business

He doesn't inherently love cleaning teeth or doing a root canal. But he does love these other things:

- Building relationships
- Teaching

- Giving advice
- Connecting
- Motivating and inspiring his team

He would tell you that he doesn't love dentistry, but he's grown to love being a dentist. How?

He applied his uniqueness to the job at hand. He connects with his patients, teaches his hygienists, motivates and inspires his team, and gives advice and counsel as asked. He prepares himself to do so every day by meditating, studying, and serving people. And this method has sustained him in a career he doesn't inherently love for more than twenty years.

Finally, the same is true for your responsibilities at home. One parent may be adept at providing organization and structure, while another parent is empathetic and compassionate. I know parents who are firm and disciplined, while others are flexible and spontaneous. Each parent is endowed with unique talents and, remember, placed in exactly the right family situation to develop and magnify those talents.

The way you lead family home evening or Come, Follow Me should be dictated by your talents. When you're having conversations around the dinner table, deploy your talents. My wife is a master nurturer, adept at creating an environment of love and harmony that opens our children up to sharing the important details of their lives. As a result, her warmth and compassion leads to greater family unity and trust.

On the other hand, I'm a facilitator who's inquisitive and loves to teach through questions. As a result, family scripture study may start by learning about repentance in Alma and end with discussions about whether or not cats will speak English in the next life.

TALENTS AND WEAKNESS

By the way, if you don't have talent in a certain area, does that excuse you from developing it? If you're not a particularly compassionate or emotional person, does that mean you should just walk the world as a "thinker," flexing your analysis on all with whom you come in contact?

No! In Doctrine and Covenants 46:8 the Lord commands his Saints to "seek ye earnestly the best gifts, always remembering for what they are given." He expects us to develop skills that we just don't have. If you aren't a great teacher but get called to teach Sunday School, have the faith to say "yes" to the calling, and then get to work developing your knowledge and skill.

Elder Richard G. Scott said, "Upward growth occurs in cycles that build upon each other in an ascending spiral of capacity and understanding. They are often not easy, but they are always beneficial. As you walk the path of righteousness, you will grow in strength, understanding, and self-esteem. **You will discover hidden talents and unknown capacities.** The whole course of your life may be altered for your happiness and the Lord's purposes."[3]

The Lord needs willing hearts and active hands to accomplish His work. In the process of developing knowledge and skill—even in areas where we feel devoid of talent—the Lord will bless our efforts for our gain. We may discover previously undiscovered talents, or we may simply struggle through a task doing the best we can. Either way, the sacrifice is honored and the blessings unfold. For those situations where you must lean into discomfort, do the best you can. But, as previously discussed, where you can use a talent to boost your energy, do it! Talents exist for the benefit of all.

LEAD WITH WHAT YOU DO BEST

Remember: at any moment of any day you are doing one of two things—either increasing your energy or draining it. There is no in between. All activities do one or the other.

One reason people lose hope, whether in work or in life, is that they are making more withdrawals than deposits. In the financial world, that's called "overdraft," which leads to fees, despair, and eventually bankruptcy.

Here's the thing: you control your deposits and withdraws. Now, this isn't true all the time. Sometimes you find yourself in a place where someone else tells you what to do, when, and where. But most of us have just enough flexibility in our lives to control what we do and in what order we do it.

Most people do what I call "stumbling into energy." Their day looks something like the graph below. The line in the middle represents a neutral state, neither positive nor negative. They start the day by checking their email, which immediately begins the energy drain. They may talk with a friend or accidentally do something they enjoy, but then they get back to checking things off their to-do list, draining their energy further. By the end of the day, no activity can get them back to equilibrium. Their energy is too far down. Again, throughout the day they may have had spikes in energy here or there, but they weren't intentional and didn't last.

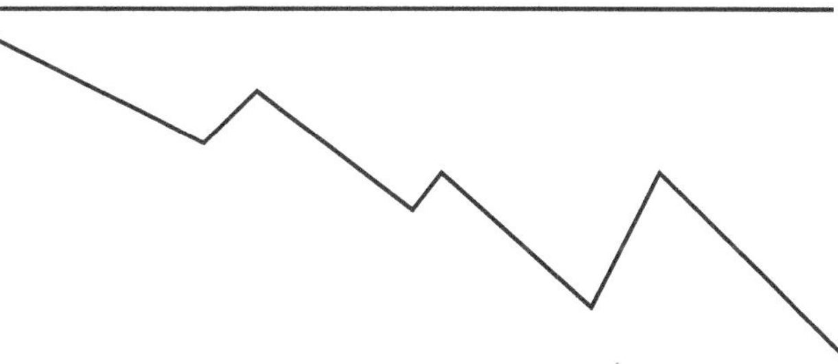

In contrast, when you lead with what you do best, you start your morning off with a spike. For example, at my last job I blocked the first thirty minutes of every day for what I called "sharpening the ax," an ode to Stephen Covey's concept of learning and sharpening my skills.

I'd read the *Harvard Business Review*, listen to a podcast, or simply read a book. Inputting this knowledge spiked my energy and helped me prep for the day. I would then make a withdrawal on that energy to do some stuff I hated, like paperwork or email follow-up or planning. Right around 11 a.m. I'd spike my energy again with a pre-scheduled coaching session with a colleague. The interaction and dynamic conversation would spike my energy (and I'd also often get to use some of the things I learned that morning). I'd then drain my energy again doing program planning or some other tedious task. Finally, I'd schedule a training, another coaching session, or simply following up on coaching by sending along my coaching notes at the end of the day. This would ensure I left the office with a smile on my face and my energy high. I'd listen to something interesting on the way home, like a podcast or NPR. I would then walk into the house feeling good rather than beat down. And that made all the difference.

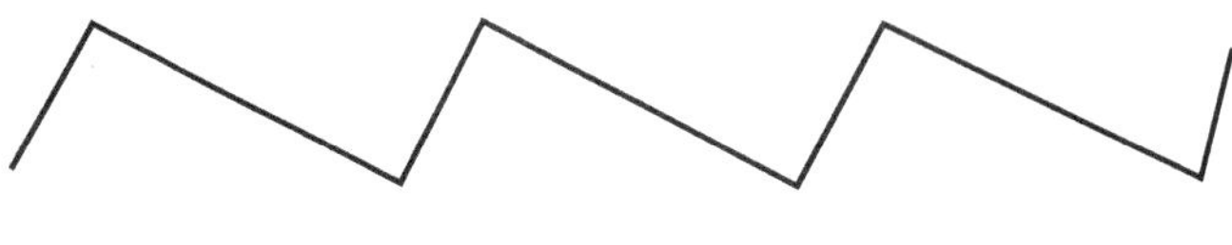

So what makes the difference between a deposit and a withdrawal?

Talents.

When you utilize your talents you release energy, satisfaction, and happiness into your world, which results in a deposit. When you work in your weakness, you drain your energy, resulting in less productivity and output and low morale.

It's important here to stop and clarify that a weakness is not something you're bad it. Rather, it's something you could be good at **but that does not give you energy.** By the way, many of us work jobs where we're paid to do things we're good at but hate doing.

The goal is to target talents.

So take a moment and reflect on the following:

- In what new situations can you put yourself to use your talents more? Who do you need to talk to?
- How can you change your schedule or the order of operations to maximize your talent?

Intentionally crafting your life is nothing more than taking the tasks you already do and reframing your experience. Get clear about the things that give you energy—and those that drain it—then organize your day to yield the greatest results!

THE PROMISE OF TALENTS

Going back to where we started, the promises of using our talents are great:

> His lord said unto him, Well done, thou good and faithful servant: thou hast been faithful over a few things, I will make thee ruler over many things: enter thou into the joy of thy lord.
>
> For unto every one that hath shall be given, and he shall have abundance: but from him that hath not shall be taken away even that which he hath. (Matthew 25: 21, 29)

The Lord promises abundance. That could mean spiritual growth, temporal gain, emotional peace, or more. There is no end to the abundance the Lord can provide. He promises that we will "rule over many things." This could mean self-discipline, a command of our environment, or simply His trust that we will be wise stewards of all that He blesses us with, whether financial, physical, or otherwise. And He promises the joy of the Lord! I don't know what all that must entail, but I've caught a glimpse of it in my life.

I left my job in public relations sixteen years ago to pursue more meaningful work. In the process, I've discovered, developed, and applied my talents to everything I've done. Centering my work on my talents has led to greater success, more resilience, and more happiness in work. Applying them in my callings has yielded greater impact and a feeling of congruence and authenticity that comes with "bringing yourself" to the calling. Utilizing them in the home has made me a better husband and father and has changed the way I lead my family in prayer, scripture study, family home evening, family council, and more. But most important, I've felt closer to the Lord. I've felt the peace of being on His errand, serving those around me in the way I think He might if He were here physically. Using talents has given me insight into who He wants me to become, and the same is true for you!

THE BEST THING YOU CAN DO FOR HUMANKIND

Perhaps you are like I was in that workshop many years ago. You've learned about talents, their origin, how to identify them, how to grow them, and, most important, how to put them to work for the benefit of all. But maybe you're sitting there asking, "Now what?" The next step is the most important.

An interesting thing happened at a high school in south Texas a few years ago. I was invited to speak to a group of two hundred graduating seniors about talents. Much like the young women mentioned at the beginning of the book, not a single one of these students believed they had talent. We dove into a two-hour session about talents—what they are, how to identify them, and how to use them to guide their search for a college major and career. By the end of the training, the energy was high, so I attempted to capitalize on the energy to hear some of their talents.

"Raise your hand if you discovered a talent over the past two hours," I said. Almost every hand went up. Two hundred or more talents discovered. "Raise your hand if you'd be willing to share your talent with the group."

All hands went down. "Whoa," I said. "Let's try that again. Raise your hand if you identified a talent." All hands back up. "Keep it up if you'll share it with the group." All hands went down.

I asked if they noticed that phenomenon. Almost everyone discovered a talent, but no one would share it. "What's up with that?" I asked. "Everyone has these innate abilities that make you unique, special, and powerful, but no one will share them. Why not?"

It was quiet for a few moments before one person spoke up.

"I'm afraid. What if I'm not actually that good at this thing?"

Another chimed in, "What if people laugh when I share it?"

Another said, "What if people don't think I'm as good at it as I think I am?"

Again, I can relate, and yet living for the Lord starts with discovering, developing, and then sharing your talents. Raise your hand! When the opportunity comes to teach a class, serve in an assignment, visit a family, volunteer, or fill any other need, raise your hand! More important, pointedly ignore the voice in your head that says there's probably someone better than you to fulfill this need.

The very thing you can do for yourself, your family, and the kingdom of God is to do what you do best *consistently* for the benefit of others.

This week—even today—commit to raise your hand and share your gifts with others. Equally important, share with others the gifts you see in them. Go talk with your spouse, friend, family member, or colleague and tell them the greatness you see in them. Then find an opportunity this week to exercise your gifts. Pray to the Lord for guidance and courage.

Then raise your hand.

We need you.

NOTES

1. James E. Faust, "I Believe I Can, I Knew I Could, October 2002, churchofjesuschrist.org/study/general-conference/2002/10/i-believe-i-can-i-knew-i-could?lang=eng.
2. Taylor, Henry D. "Gifts and Talents." *New Era* (August 1977). Web.
3. Richard G. Scott, in Conference Report, Apr. 1991, 43; or *Ensign*, May 1991, 34; emphasis added.

About the Author

Dustin Peterson has led high-impact leadership training and career coaching for more than fifteen years. He is the founder and CEO at Proof Leadership Group, a leadership consultancy focused on building outstanding cultures where people thrive. He has helped more than 120 companies and thousands of individuals do more of what they do best as a trainer, coach, and consultant in the private, public, and nonprofit sectors.

Dustin completed his MS in educational leadership from Indiana University and his BS in communications at Brigham Young University–Idaho. He is the author of *Reset: How to Get Paid and Love What You Do* and lives in Houston with his wife and four kids.

You can connect with Dustin at dustin@proofleadership.com, via Instagram @proofleadership, or by visiting his site at www.proofleadership.com.

Notes

Notes

Notes